ONE CORNER C

All good wishes

Joanna Bogle

ONE CORNER OF LONDON

A history of St Bede's church, Clapham Park

Joanna Bogle

GRACEWING

First published in 2003

Gracewing
2 Southern Avenue, Leominster
Herefordshire HR6 0QF

ISBN 0 85244 579 2

Typeset by Action Publishing Technology Ltd,
Gloucester GL1 5SR

Printed by Antony Rowe Ltd
Eastbourne BN23 6QT

Foreword

by Rt Rev Mgr Richard Moth, Vicar-General, Diocese of Southwark

The centenary of a parish is always a great event and this short history of St Bede's is a timely addition to the celebrations. It chronicles the life of a parish, of a community of people living out their Catholic Faith in succeeding generations. There is much joy in this history – an account of a growing and vibrant community.

Joanna Bogle has done the parish a great service in providing this history, written in a lively and informative style.

A history such as this is not only about rejoicing in those who have gone before and have formed the community of today. It should also be an encouragement for the future. May this Centenary Year be a time of grace for the people, priests and religious of St Bede's, as the community continues to proclaim the Gospel in the years that lie ahead.

Mgr Richard Moth, VG
(Assistant Priest, St Bede's, 1982–1985)

A history of
St Bede's church

One hundred years ago, this corner of South London had no cars, and the people who lived here had no television sets, had never heard any pop music and wore clothes that would seem to us elaborately formal. They were mostly English people although some were Irish. Few, if any, had ever met anyone from Africa or the West Indies, Pakistan, or Bengal. No one here had ever heard of pizza, or a Macdonalds hamburger, or seen a lorry or an aeroplane. If you had told them that some would live to see men land on the moon or that Britain would have a woman Prime Minister, or that the British Empire would disappear, they would have considered you absurd.

A history of this one parish, Clapham Park, reflects all the changes that have affected ordinary people in Britain during the twentieth century. It is a history worth recording, bringing together many personal family stories and showing the steady passing on of the Catholic Faith through one particular church, dedicated to St Bede – himself a distinguished historian whose writings helped to ensure a continuity of faith in our country.

The story begins with a child born in 1846 – Frances Elizabeth Ellis, one of two daughters born into a prosperous family who came originally from Birkenhead. She was brought up in great comfort in a house run by a large staff. Her only sister was gravely handicapped, and Frances was to spend her life taking care of her. When her parents died, Frances, who never married, inherited a substantial

1

fortune. She was to give most of it away. Always devout, she became a Catholic in 1903. This was the start of her generous gifts to the Church – in all she was to donate about £14 million (in today's money). She was particularly generous to the Diocese of Southwark, where she paid for churches to be built in many of the London suburbs. In the year that she converted, she donated the freehold of a major property, Hyde House, in Thornton Road, Clapham Park. It cost £3,000. It was – and is – a substantial house, built in the early nineteenth century, with a large basement, imposing entrance hall and staircase, substantial reception rooms on the first floor, and a number of bedrooms and offices. Today it is the presbytery of St Bede's church, home to a number of clergy, and headquarters of St Bede's parish. It is with this house that the story of St Bede's parish begins.

At the beginning of the nineteenth century, Clapham Park had several such large houses, built in what had become a pleasant prosperous suburb with a semi-rural atmosphere, a few miles south of London. Hyde House was set back from the road, with a pleasant garden in front and a large plot of land at the back and alongside. Clapham Park parish can be proud of its link with Frances Ellis, and it is intriguing that the year of the parish's foundation was the year of her own reception into the Catholic Church and of her life's work of generosity in the founding of parishes. The date of her reception into the Catholic Church was 8 January 1903, with Sister Iphegenie, of the Daughters of the Cross, acting as her sponsor and godmother. Sister Iphegenie, a German nun, had come to Britain to help establish Catholic schools and finally became the Sister Provincial in charge of all the members of her order in Britain. She first met Miss Ellis when the latter was living at Ramsgate, and Sister was visiting a sanatorium run by the Daughters of the Cross at Margate nearby. The two women became friends and colleagues in a number of projects to help the poor and sick, notably the establishment of a hospital in Cornwall in a house which Miss Ellis owned there.

2

Miss Ellis' gift, in the year of her reception into the Church, was to create a new Catholic parish in a corner of London, although this was not the clear plan at the time. In fact, the original scheme was to use the house as a school. On 8 September 1903 Bishop Francis Bourne, the Bishop of Southwark, celebrated Mass in the house, in a room on the ground floor that had been converted into a chapel. The chapel was dedicated to St John Berchmans, a young Jesuit student saint (1599–1621) who had been chosen as the patron of the school, a junior house for the diocesan seminary at Wonersh in Surrey. St John Berchmans was patron of the junior boys at Wonersh. The Bishop himself had been the first rector of the seminary when it was founded at Henfield in Sussex in 1889. The opening of this junior house in Clapham Park was evidently seen as a useful extension of the whole work of the seminary, and was also a good way of making use of the unusually large premises which Miss Ellis had donated to the diocese. Bishop Bourne had planned to live at the house, and oversee the running of the school and its links with the seminary. But this was not to be. This opening Mass in September 1903 was in fact Bourne's last official act as Bishop of Southwark – just three days later he became Archbishop of Westminster, and later a cardinal. This meant that he would be the effective leader of all the Catholic bishops of England and Wales and a figure of national importance. He moved to his new home across the river in London SW1. But his heart remained in Southwark and, especially, with the seminary. In a speech made not long after his appointment to Westminster, he mentioned the many letters of congratulation his new appointment had brought but added 'Many, however, of the writers thought only of the added dignity and little of the bitter pain the separation from Seminary and diocese causes me.' He never really wanted to leave Southwark and, as we will see, he was to have a continuing link with this parish of Clapham Park.

The school, operating as a junior house for boys planning to become priests, was soon busy. By the end of 1903 the first pupils had arrived and the rector was Fr Gerald Fitzgibbon. He had been on the staff at Wonersh, and some of the pupils from the youngest class at Wonersh in due course were also moved over to Hyde House. We have the names of some of those who were educated at Hyde House during this period. They include Frs John Franklin, Thomas Smith, James O'Connell, Aloysius Phillips, Hubert Gibney (later Monsignor Gibney, Vicar-General of the diocese), Harold Knight and Thomas Cambourne. Others at school here were Reginald Darnley, Bernard McCourt, Francis Shephard, Willian Ryan, Arthur Henderson, James Yiend, Leonard Charney, Percy Flavin, John Sliney, Joseph Mariani, David Barry, and J. Harris.

A note in the history archives at Archbishop's House, Southwark (probably compiled in the 1920s) says:

There were very few people living in this neighbourhood when we started in 1903, but Miss Ellis, our great benefactress, gave us a good property called Hyde House and the then Bishop thought that Mass might be said in the first floor of the house for the Catholics who might be found there and that the house might be used as a small school for boys especially such as might be likely candidates for the priesthood. He became Archbishop [ie of Westminster] just at this time, but he had selected Fr Gerald Fitzgibbon from the staff at Wonersh seminary for this work. Fr Fitzgibbon came in September 1903 with Mr John Haffenden who was beginning his studies for the priesthood at St Augustine's Walworth. Fr Fitzgibbon broke down in health in January 1905 and a deacon, Leo Bourdelot came from Wonersh to help. Very few boys availed themselves of the school and it was closed in Easter 1905.

During this time the diocese acquired a new bishop, replacing Bishop Bourne who had gone to Westminster. He was Bishop Peter Amigo, a Gibraltarian by birth, who was to rule over the Diocese of Southwark for more than fifty years. He came to Hyde House a few days before he was consecrated as bishop in 1904, in order to make a private retreat before taking on the new and important responsibilities of the Diocese.

The Catholic Directory for 1904 lists under 'Clapham Park, SW':

> St John Berchmans, Hyde House, Thornton Rd. Temporary Chapel in school. Rev G. Fitzgibbon.

There was Sunday Mass at 8 a.m. and 10 a.m., devotions and Benediction at 7 p.m., with Mass on Holydays at 8 a.m. and on ordinary weekdays at 7 a.m. Confessions were on Saturdays from 7 p.m. to 9 p.m.

Although the little school closed, Hyde House continued to be used as part of St John's seminary. The history archive note continues:

> From September 1905 to July 1907 we tried to make use of the house for the lowest class of the seminary then called Rudiments, and we had 16 boys the first year under Fr Michael Hanlon and Fr Westlake. Fr Hanlon went back to Wonersh in Sept 1906 and Fr Arthur Armstrong took charge, but the class was smaller the second year. Fr Armstrong himself was required at Wonersh, and it was decided to discontinue having Rudiments here from July 1907.

During these early years of the twentieth century, the Church in Britain faced what became known as 'The Modernist Crisis', which affected the Diocese of Southwark as it centred on a Southwark priest, Fr George Tyrell. His unorthodox views – especially on the nature of Christ, which appeared to question Christ's divinity – brought him into conflict with the Church and with the Bishop of Southwark in particular. In retrospect, this was a crisis which – although it was controlled at the time through the discipline of the Church – was perhaps a foretaste of things to come, when many central doctrines of the Catholic Faith were to be challenged in the 1960s and 70s, in the years following the Second Vatican Council.

The modernism crisis affected the seminary and the training and formation of priests, and would have been much discussed at Hyde House. The house was essentially an extension of the Wonersh seminary and a centre of study – not yet an ordinary parish.

St Bede's has always been rather proud of this link with Wonersh seminary and with the men who studied here who subsequently went on to become priests. But Fr Hanlon, while running the Rudiments class, was also busy with plans to establish a real parish church here, as the chapel in Hyde House was obviously much too small for any growing local Catholic community. On 4 November 1905, the foundation stone of St Bede's church was laid, on the land alongside Hyde House, fronting onto Thornton Road. The church would be of a simple and plain design, like all the churches funded by Miss Ellis (they were sometimes known as 'Ellis boxes'!) across the Diocese of Southwark. The building work did not take long. It was completed by the spring, and on 26 April 1906 the church was opened by the new Bishop of Southwark, Bishop Peter Amigo. It could accommodate more than 200 worshippers and had cost in excess of £2,000 – a sum that had to be borrowed, incurring a parish debt which would be gradually paid off in the ensuing years. The local newspaper, *The Clapham Observer*, reported on the opening ceremony:

> The new Roman Catholic Church, dedicated to St Bede, and erected in Thornton Road, Clapham Park, was duly opened for public worship last Friday April 27th, although the erection of the organ gallery and other matters remain still to be completed. Plain even to the point of severity almost in its architectural and other features, the building provides accommodation for some 250 worshippers.

On 15 April 1908 the parish was formally registered under the law as 'a Place of Meeting for Religious Worship', the relevant document – still in the parish archives – being signed by Fr George Newton. Two years later came the registration of the building for the solemnization of marriages, with a formal certificate from the local (Wandsworth) Registrar: from now on, the parish priest at Clapham Park could use the building for weddings. (Many years later, with the reorganization of the London Boroughs, St Bede's, to most people's regret, came under the jurisdiction of Lambeth).

It is not clear why the name of St Bede's was chosen. Bede, often known as The Venerable, has no local connection with this part of England at all. He was born in Northumbria towards the end of the seventh century, and became a monk at Jarrow, spending his whole life there. He became a noted biblical scholar but his chief importance is as an historian; he wrote the *History of the English Church and People* which recorded for us the early centuries of our nation's life. Perhaps he was chosen as patron of this London suburban parish simply because he was an English saint.

Fr Hanlon, as we have seen, was needed back at Wonersh so he was replaced as rector by Fr (later Monsignor) Arthur Armstrong, who was assisted by Fr Charles Westlake. During Fr Armstrong's time as parish priest, he arranged for a stable adjoining Hyde House to be converted into a parish hall. The following year, Fr Armstrong was himself replaced by Fr George Newton, who was parish priest for only one year. A leaflet telling the history of St Bede's, published in 1932, notes:

After so many changes it was hoped Father Newton would remain for a considerable time and when, in 1908, the Bishop wished to appoint him Vice-Rector of the Seminary, his Lordship kindly expressed to the people his own regret at having to move their Rector. He explained it was due to his need of the best man in the diocese for the work of the Seminary. He then appointed Father Westlake as Rector, and said he would leave him at St Bede's for many, many years to come.

In fact, tragically Fr Newton was not to remain for very long at Wonersh Seminary – he died only four years later, in 1912.

The parish was busy enough to have various active groups, and one was the Sodality of Our Lady, established in 1904 during Fr Westlake's time there. The document – all written in Latin – formally establishing the Sodality was signed by the Bishop in 1908. It consisted of a rather impressive printed form, in which the details of the local Sodality were added in handwriting. Interestingly, four years after his appointment, Bishop Peter Amigo was still using the old forms printed for his predecessor, Francis Bourne, and on this particular form, the name 'Franciscus' and his coat of arms have been crossed through in blue pencil, and the name 'Petrus' substituted.

Fr Westlake was already well known in the parish after three years as curate. In addition to taking on his new duties as parish priest, he was keen to re-establish Hyde House as a school, and wrote to the Bishop several times about this. The pressure for such a school seems to have come from parents who thought that the nearby Catholic schools for boys, Clapham College, was unsuitable for middle-class children. This was a tension which would continue for several years – evidently for some reason some families simply considered Clapham College too 'mixed' (to use their coy phrase) for their offspring. In writing to the Bishop with his plans, Fr Westlake seems not to have been deterred by the small number of boys who attended Hyde House while it was a junior seminary, for there is no mention of this in his letters. In October 1908 he wrote to the Bishop:

Has your Lordship ever thought of starting in a small way [this last phrase is underlined in the original] a higher class preparatory school for boys before they go to college? One that would take a class of boy superior to the mixed class at Clapham College and therefore one that would not become antagonistic to the latter's interests. I have had the suggestion put forward by several ladies living near here at Streatham and from what I know I am rather inclined to think the plan is possible. There are several Protestant schools in Streatham which take a certain number of our boys, because the parents think Clapham and even Wimbledon now, too mixed and also too far away. I am only throwing out the suggestion as of course it would mean a good deal of forethought. All to whom I have spoken seem most favourable to the idea. In any case the Catholic boys round Streatham of that class are not provided for.

I am now occupied in teaching one boy of eleven the Our Father, Hail Mary etc which he has forgotten through going to Protestant schools for the last three years.

Offering full apologies for writing such a long letter, I remain.

Your lordship's obedient servant in Deo,
Charles M. Westlake.

PS. I think it could be worked without calling on the diocese for a single penny.

The financial costs of such a school were evidently much on his mind, as he wrote again to the Bishop the following month saying that his mother had promised £300 for the project if he needed it 'for the preliminary expenses.' He pleaded again for this school, and clearly felt that he was putting the Bishop under too much pressure, for the letter concludes 'I must close up now or else you will have an excuse to take another glass of claret at dinner after such a long scribble.' But the Xaverians, who were running Clapham College, were also busily lobbying the Bishop. Convinced that any proposed school at Clapham Park would damage their school by drawing away potential pupils, they put their own case strongly. In December Fr Westlake was writing again to the Bishop: 'Fr Warwick came on Sunday ... I concluded Fr Warwick came to advise me on your behalf and to let me know Fr Cuthbert's objection to the proposed school. I therefore spoke quite openly to him about all matters ... He is against it in every way, and thinks it will be in opposition to Clapham College whether we mean it or no ...'

The school project came to nothing, and Fr – later Canon – Westlake was not to remain much longer at St Bede's, as he was, like his predecessors, required at Wonersh as a teacher. He was replaced in 1909 by Fr Thomas Hooley. He was to be parish priest here for many years and to put his stamp on St Bede's and on the neighbourhood. Born in December 1876 and ordained in 1899 at Wonersh, Fr Hooley, who like his predecessors had been on the staff at Wonersh, had a strong academic background and had studied in Rome. He was always known as Dr Hooley. He was to make his mark on the parish and to become a well-known local character, as he remained as parish priest for over forty years.

Not long after Dr Hooley's appointment, Fr Cornelius O'Donohue, who had just been ordained and was continuing his studies at London University, came to live in the parish and helped with the Sunday Masses. He left when his academic studies were over. Later, Canon St John came to live at Hyde House and give similar help, remaining until 1913 when he was appointed as chaplain to Walton Prison, Liverpool.

The question of a school for boys continued to be discussed back and forth over the next few years, and in 1910 Dr Hooley was writing to the Bishop pointing out that such a project would 'also provide a solution to the constant struggle of what to do with this enormous house. I know that the Xaverian brothers at Clapham would object, but if I started a school it would not be in competition with them. A school for boys is certainly a need in this neighbourhood, and with a few boarders could be made to support itself ...' The next year he sent the Bishop a list of twelve boys, all at non-Catholic schools, who would probably become pupils if a school were to be founded. It was to no avail as the project never got off the ground.

An urgent need was a parish elementary school for the children of the ordinary working families, and this was a project which did receive official blessing. With this in mind in September 1910 Dr Hooley issued a letter appealing for funds:

The steady increase in the number of Catholics in the district (the average attendance at Mass on Sunday is over 300) has made the provision of an Elementary School for younger children an absolute necessity, and this has been made possible through the kindness of the nuns at La Retraite Convent, who have undertaken to do the teaching gratuitously.

The Hall beside the Presbytery has been converted into an excellent school-room, suitable for about 40 children, with cloak-room and everything necessary for an up-to-date schoolroom. These alterations have been made at a cost of £33.10s., and the necessary equipment has cost nearly £20. So the New School has involved an initial expenditure of £50. To meet this, a sum of £28 has been raised, of which amount only £6.10s. has come from the congregation. A year ago the capital debt on the Church amounted to £2,330 11s. 6d. This amount has been reduced by £65, and the year's interest, which came to nearly £94, has been paid. This heavy debt should prevent any further obligations being undertaken, but the imminent danger to the Faith of a number of children, through attending Non-Catholic Schools on account of there being no Catholic School in the district, is a sufficient reason to ask the Congregation to make a special effort to start the New School.

I earnestly ask all who can help in this matter by contributing something towards the £22 yet required.

Members of the Congregation are invited to visit the School and judge for themselves the value and necessity of the work being done.

The first headmistress of this school was Mother Imelda who came, as we have seen, from La Retraite convent. She ran the school for five years, and was succeeded by Mother St Edith, who was to be headmistress for the next quarter of a century. Many years later she was to contribute her reminiscences to a parish publication:

Cardinal Bourne gave his blessing to the work. Desks and tables, old-fashioned ones, were hunted up. The whole place was painted yellow and a small cloakroom, fitted with pegs and two washing basins, was to serve as a recreation room when the weather was wet. Eventually the LCC [London County Council – then the education authority for London] was to approve it for 50 infants. Of course the two classes that we had were held in the same room, though later on they were separated by a curtain. Some of the more prosperous Catholic families paid a weekly shilling or two to help with the general expenses. Under modern requirements our poor little school could not have long existed.

La Retraite Convent in Atkins Road had been founded in 1880 and the sisters were, over the years, to play a large part in the life of St Bede's parish. The school had extensive grounds and gardens and offered an almost rural setting for the girls being educated there. The nuns were from a French teaching order, and although the school was in many ways a very typical English girls' school of its day, it had some French touches and traditions which were to linger over the years.

It is notable that Mother St Edith mentions Cardinal Bourne, rather than the Bishop of Southwark, Bishop Amigo, in her reminiscences. There is an intriguing background to this. Cardinal Bourne was a great friend of the parish priest, Dr Hooley, and came to see him every week. Dr Hooley was in fact the Cardinal's confessor. Naturally not every ordinary South London parish has a cardinal coming to visit every week, so the parishioners of Clapham Park were rather proud of this link. But it did create some tensions in the wider Church, because Cardinal Bourne was now Archbishop of Westminster. It was in one sense unusual that he would cross the river and leave his own diocese regularly each week and enter the Diocese of Southwark. Although these visits were for purely personal spiritual reasons – he was seeing his confessor – his presence naturally evoked comment. The two dioceses are not really equal in rank – Westminster is the chief diocese in England because it includes the capital city with all the most important administrative centres of the nation: Parliament, the home of the Royal Family, all the Government offices, the central commercial structures, the headquarters of all the main newspapers. Southwark straddles the south bank of the river Thames and is essentially residential and commercial, covering all the southern London suburbs and large parts of rural and semi-rural Surrey and Kent.

In addition to these regular visits to see Dr Hooley, the Cardinal made a formal visit on St Bede's Day in May 1912, which happened that year to be Whit Monday. Canon St John celebrated a special High Mass which the Cardinal attended.

Cardinal Bourne had a long-running dispute with Southwark's Bishop Amigo as Bourne was keen to merge Southwark Diocese with that of Westminster and was endlessly plotting and planning for this 'takeover' bid, even writing to Rome and making visits there to build up a lobby to support his claims. It seems that, because of Dr Hooley's friendship with the Cardinal, St Bede's was a small pocket of 'pro-Bourne' opinion within the Diocese of Southwark where most of the priests obviously tended to side with their own Bishop and to defend the claims of Southwark as an independent entity. In fact, Bourne's

13

attempts to lay claim to the Southwark Diocese, although ultimately crushed by Rome, continued throughout the First World War – when the authorities in Rome, like everyone else, certainly had other things on their minds! – and again in 1921 and 1925.

But none of this prevented the parish from flourishing, and Dr Hooley officially reported to his own Bishop in all formal matters. Then, as now, every parish had to make regular reports to the bishop giving details of the church building, the school, the finances of the parish, etc. These 'Visitation returns' give some flavour of state of things at Clapham Park during those years. In 1908 in reply to the question 'Is any part of the Fabric out of repair?' the reply was 'Yes; porch of house is underpinned. Damp coming in upper rooms.' Receipts for the year to 30 June 1908 were 'sittings £25 – 3 – 1. Offertories £73-18-2'. (The amounts are of course, given in pounds, shillings, and pence, the pre-decimal currency). One question which looks puzzling to modern eyes is 'What and how much accommodation is reserved for the Poor at Sunday Masses?' This refers to the custom of 'pew rents' in which wealthier families could pay to have the regular use of a pew – other parts of the church were open to anyone, i.e. allocated for the poor. At St Bede's, most of the church was evidently available for the poor as the response is 'charge for only a few at Sunday Masses'. But those who could pay made a valuable contribution to the parish, as the 'sittings' sum indicated under the receipts above indicates. It is also interesting to note that the church was not yet registered for marriages, as in response to the question 'Have you the certificate of licence for your Church?' the reply is 'Not yet but being applied for.'

In 1911 St Bede's held a Parish Mission, which was evidently a great success as the Bishop wrote to Dr Hooley in April, 'I am very glad to know that the Mission has been such a great success and I congratulate you and your people on the good attendance at the services.'

These years of the 1900s were a time of steady growth at

St Bede's. By 1912 the parish organizations included the Guild of the Blessed Sacrament, Children of Mary, the Apostleship of Prayer, the St Vincent de Paul Society and the Third Order of St Francis, and the average Mass attendance had risen to 350. It is also worthy of note that the pew-rent system had evidently by then been abolished as in answer to the question 'What free accommodation is there at each of the Sunday Masses?' the response was 'The whole church.'

Clapham Park was by now something of a bustling suburb, losing its semi-rural flavour. Motor cars were now occasionally seen, along with buses and trams. But in appearance the area still had something of the nineteenth century about it. Women wore skirts that trailed on the ground, and they rarely went out without a hat. Children wore dark clothes and those of the poorer classes were usually shod in substantial boots. In residential areas, away from the main highways, it was still safe to play in the centre of the road and children ran about there with their hoops, stopping to allow traffic – usually a horse-drawn tradesman's vehicle – to pass by. Most middle-class families had at least a cook and general maid-of-all-work to help run the house and this was the normal job that a teenage girl expected on leaving school. There was an atmosphere of stability about life – although a new century had opened, and the Edwardian era had begun following the death of Queen Victoria in 1901, for most people life was not dramatically different from that of their grandparents.

While the parish of St Bede's was being established, another institution which was to play a big part in local life was also being born.

A house called St Hugh's, opposite St Bede's in Clapham Park, was the home of Mr Norman Potter, a wealthy Londoner who was a convert to Catholicism. From here, he ran a number of projects. In 1899 he opened a boys' club for youngsters living in the areas of poverty along the south banks of the Thames. The club aimed to offer sporting, recreational, and other facilities within the context of the Catholic faith and by 1906 it was well established as the Fisher Club at Bermondsey. Mr Potter also sought to care for orphans, and for youngsters who for one reason or another lacked proper families and needed somewhere to live, and St Hugh's – a large house similar to Hyde House – was turned into a full-scale boys' home.

Mr Potter was evidently a man of great devotion, and also great energy. From the start, St Hugh's had a strong spiritual base, with its own chapel and its own life of prayer and shared activities.

In fact Mr Potter took the extraordinary and unusual step of personally adopting a large number of boys, and even giving them his own surname. He took full responsibility for their care while young and for helping them establish themselves in jobs as they grew older. From his home at St Hugh's a huge range of other activities were also run: by 1912 these included, according to the list printed on its letterhead: 'St Francis' Cottage, St Gerard's Home, St Laurence's Home, The Fisher Institute (a) Marine Street Club (b) Vienna Road Club'. Not all of these were actually in Clapham Park – St Laurence's was at Tankerton in Kent and was a holiday home for the Clapham children.

Although these had been established with Mr Potter's money, they needed day-to-day funds, and there were regular events to raise these, and to arouse interest in St Hugh's. A handbill for 1911 announces a special stall in aid of St Hugh's at the Catholic Charity Bazaar held at the Portman Rooms, Baker Street (admission one shilling – 5p in today's currency). The stall had evidently attracted the support of several well-known authors, who had donated books – the list reads like a 'Who's Who' of Edwardian authors:

AT OUR STALL in addition to the ordinary articles sold at a Bazaar we have a special feature in the form of Books. We have many specially inscribed by their

16

authors, with books by the following: Mr Rudyard Kipling, Fr Maturin, Miss Rhoda Broughton, Mgr Benson, Fr Bearne SJ, Mr and Mrs Egerton Cole, Abbot Gasquet, Mother Salome, Mr A. C. Benson, Mr Hilaire Belloc, Hon Maurice Baring, Mrs Belloc Lowndes, Mr Edmund Gardner.

St Hugh's was a substantial house on the corner of Thornton Road and Kings Avenue, with its official address usually given as 129 Kings Avenue, but sometimes as Thornton Road. Letterheaded paper for 1910 carries the telephone number '704 Streatham'. To have a telephone would have been quite unusual at that time. The letterhead also carries the information that the nearest underground station is Balham, (this is still the case) and also 'Electric trams: alight at Dinsmore Road, Balham' (perhaps re-introducing this tram would solve our modern traffic problems in and around Clapham Park!).

This letter was to request permission for a retreat to be held at St Hugh's, under the direction of a Fr Goodier, a Jesuit from 'Manresa' the Jesuit house at Roehampton (Fr Goodyear was later Archbishop of Bombay): 'The Retreat will be for my own family of boys, St Gerard's boys and St Joseph's boys, and any other of our own boys who can get into the chapel and who are old enough to appreciate it.'

Another project was St Vincent's, a home for children with health problems. This was run by Mr Potter in association with the Sisters of Charity. It was run on unusual lines, in that the boys slept in a dormitory which, although roofed, was essentially out of doors and open on three sides to the elements. The boys, many of whom had serious handicaps and were confined to bed, seem nevertheless to have thrived under this regime, with colds and flu and asthma being unknown among them. In cold weather, they were given hot water bottles, extra blankets, balaclava helmets and warm gloves each night!

The boys' homes became extremely well known, and

17

attracted support from fashionable patrons, including royalty. Mr Potter made good use of the fact that the work was in London, and thus highly accessible to the rich and famous. He published booklets and pamphlets describing the activities of the various homes, and waxed lyrical about what went on there. A booklet published in 1910 described in detail 'A Day with a Franciscan Household', in which Mr Potter, who was a Franciscan tertiary (i.e. a lay person who is associated with the Franciscan Order although not bound by its vows), took the reader on a tour of his various houses and projects. After describing how the household at St Hugh's rose early, for daily Mass at 6.30 a.m. followed by breakfast and the departure of the boys to school or work, he took the reader to his desk for a look at the day's letters: requests for help from impoverished families or from men out of work, donations for the various projects, medical reports concerning the patients at St Vincents.

Language changes over the years, and whereas today we refer to handicapped people, a century ago it was quite normal to use the word 'cripple', and it carried no derogatory meaning at all. On the other hand, Mr Potter's rather sentimental tone when describing the young patients at the homes is somewhat cloying, even by the standards of his day, and perhaps gives us some insight into his character:

A walk of five minutes will bring us to a very suburban looking house. This is St Joseph's, the Home of the elder crippled working boys [the full address was 139 Kings Avenue]. A man and his wife are in charge. On the right we enter the Tailor's Shop, where some nine or ten boys – in true tailor-like fashion – are sitting cross-legged on a raised platform, and are being initiated into the mysteries of tailoring. The busy hum of sewing machines is heard, and a goodly array of clothes for mending, and suits in all stages of formation are hung around. For what is the use of a Cripples' Home unless

18

the boys who are there received are taught to earn their own living and take their place in life equally with their able-bodied brothers?

On the left is the boys' playroom: a bagatelle table, books, newspapers, some bright pictures and a cosy fire complete the picture as we enter. A different scene at night time when the boys have done their work and are gathered round the fire and have their games or books, with a tune from the piano to accompany them; but it is work-time now and at St Joseph's we believe in serious work.

Through another room we come to the little Oratory, whose dignified furniture was given by a good benefactor. Here all the boys gather morning and night for their prayers, and on certain days for instruction by the Chaplain. Everything in the chapel is devotional and simple. There is nothing gaudy or tawdry, but from that little place is breathed a spirit of solid piety which is beginning to permeate the household.

Upstairs are the bedrooms, where the windows are removed so that even those who are not actually under medical treatment may still gain the benefits of the open-air regime ...

It is only a walk of about four minutes across the road to St Vincent's, our surgical home for crippled boys undergoing treatment. This is a much larger house with grounds of nearly ten acres. A splendid though somewhat small football field comes into view, which has the appearance of being well used. Across the ground we soon see the long open-air Sanatorium containing thirty beds. Every one of these beds is filled, not only, alas, at night-time but in most cases throughout the day as well, for here are the saddest little sufferers of all, though from their bright and smiling faces and cheerful songs and merry chatter they do not, indeed, give one the idea of sadness. These are the boys, young and old, who are undergoing medical treatment and who will soon, we hope, be cured. Poor little suffering members of the

19

Body of Christ! Some of them have spent many years in hospitals, and some are the little waifs and strays of our great cities sent from the Unions [i.e. the workhouses] ... What work is entailed in that roomy open-air dormitory few who do not witness it day by day can realise. Sometimes one boy is sufficient to employ a nurse the whole day and yes, even night as well. Constant care, patient nursing and hourly attention are lavished upon them. The boys never seem to feel the cold of their open-air environment. At night they have hot-water bottles and plenty of blankets, sometimes woollen helmets and gloves, but only in the coldest weather, and we never have anything in the way of colds or sore throats or whooping cough among these children. [Maybe modern families, with their sealed windows and central heating and serious problems with asthma and colds among their children should take note!]

As we pay our visit and have a chat with these little patients, we notice that some of the boys are having lessons while they are in bed, others are being massaged by the nurses, a row of boys are making woollen mats, another is painting, for even in bed idleness is not to be allowed ...

Next to be visited is the 'St Crispin's Boot Shop' where boys are taught to mend and make boots, and then a new home, St Gerard's, for destitute boys. Then, after a trip by train to see the holiday home established at Whitstable, there is time to see the depot at Kensington, where the items made by the boys are on sale to the public.

After some reflections on the importance of Christian charity, and the huge needs to be fulfilled, the booklet concludes:

The founder of this great work well remembers some ten years ago, when the little effort was in its earliest infancy, an old and honoured friend putting his hand upon his shoulder and saying 'If you are going to undertake work like this, prepare to have your heart broken many times.' The truth of that prophesy has indeed been fulfilled. The work is one of many disappointments, bitter and heart-breaking, but on the other hand there are wonderful consolations and even in this life it is sometimes permitted to one to see something of the results which, however, it is not part of our work to look for ...

Tragically, Norman Potter was to know much greater heartbreak than he could at that time have imagined. But in 1910 the future seemed full of happy prospects, and the booklet concluded with a list of 'Fifty Ways of Helping' which ranged from giving time to look after the boys in the evenings or to teach them during the day, to donating blankets, clothes, and jumble for jumble sales, arranging trips to the zoo or Madame Tussauds, giving 'lantern slides' or other entertainment, lending 'a motor or carriage occasionally, for instance to bring a crippled child to us, or take one of our speakers to a meeting' or giving bicycles to save fares or pictures or religious statues for the houses.

The patrons of St Hugh's included the Bishop of South-wark and several other bishops and the committee included representatives of the Bishops of Southwark and Westminster plus various Catholic notables. St Vincent's Home, although founded and established by Mr Potter, was under the care of the Sisters of Charity of St Vincent de Paul and had its own management. In fact correspondence shows there were many tensions and arguments between Potter and the working committee.

Mr Potter must have been a man of extraordinary energy and commitment, and was definitely somewhat eccentric. One of his closest friends was Mgr Robert Hugh Benson, the son of a former Archbishop of Canterbury. Robert Hugh Benson had caused a stir by becoming a Catholic and being ordained as a Catholic priest. He was by this time a noted author. His books about the Reformation including *Come Rack, Come Rope!* are still read today, and he also wrote some sentimental novels which have

21

been deservedly forgotten. His contribution to the life of the Catholic Church in Britain was immense, and his account of his conversion (reprinted as recently as 1990 in paperback) still has considerable relevance. His friendship with Norman Potter dated back to the time when both were Anglicans. It seems likely that he was the friend who spoke of the heartbreak that would necessarily be part of the work for the poor and sick.

In 1914 disaster struck, just at a time when the whole of Europe was embarking on the greater tragedy of the outbreak of the Great War – that horrific four years of slaughter which was to mark the destiny of Europe for a century and to bring sorrow to homes across the entire world.

At some stage in the late summer of 1914 a boy at St Hugh's told the authorities that Mr Potter had committed an act of indecency with him. Naturally, there was shock and dismay. When summoned, Mr Potter seems to have been confused and offended, and to have given a poor account of himself. A number of key people involved with the homes, including those reporting to the Bishop, became convinced of his guilt.

Extraordinarily, at just this time, Mr Potter had in fact announced his engagement, and in the midst of all the turmoil, he was married to Marie, a young woman who seems to have been associated with him in his work and to be happy to take on his entire adopted family. The ceremony was conducted by Mgr Benson and there was a traditional reception. The new Mrs Potter seems to have shown every sign of happily looking forward to a future family life.

Things seemed to be proceeding normally – in fact Mr Potter published a leaflet *St Hugh's in War-Time*, giving his supporters the latest news of his work. It included letters from his adopted sons, now serving at the Front. These make touching reading and seem to affirm that the young men had been happy at St Hugh's Home and looked back with fondness on cheerful evenings round the fire and homely chats with their adopted father. The leaflet made the usual appeal for funds, and gave news of St Vincent's and other projects. But doom was at hand. At some stage in the autumn of 1914 Mr Potter was suddenly ousted from his position, and summarily obliged to leave not only St Hugh's but England altogether. He fled with his wife to Switzerland and the whole of his work – the boys' homes, the clubs, the tailoring and shoe-making classes, were at one swoop taken over and put in the care of the diocesan authorities.

St Vincent's was left virtually untouched as it had for some years been run by the Sisters of Charity and was thus left to continue as before. But everything else was closed down and completely reorganized. It seems possible that poor Potter was in fact the victim of a smear campaign by those who had long been envious of his work.

What seems very remarkable is that all the boys at St Hugh's Home – or at least the vast majority of them – unanimously supported Mr Potter and indeed affirmed his complete innocence of any wrong doing. They were all contacted by the chaplain at the Home, Fr Frederick Orosg, and asked if anything untoward had ever taken place involving Potter.

A letter from one of them, by this time serving with the Army, survives, and is an oddly moving document. Private L. A. Potter of B Company, 8th Battalion, the Royal Fusiliers, wrote from Sandling Camp in Kent (spelling and punctuation are as in the original):

We are expected to go to the front before long, and one never knows if one will see dear old home again.

The question you put to me I can only answer with a big NO. In fact the question has rather astounded me. How anyone could make such a wicked attack on Dad I really dont know. You can immagine how much I feel it when I hear him attacked in such a way, because his life has been spent in trying to make us good, true minded men.

23

Fr Orosg also summoned all the boys then currently living at St Hugh's, and asked them the same question. The result was a statement signed by them, which they gave him to be passed on to the diocesan authorities. It is rather touching to see the large collection of names, all bearing the surname Potter. Can they really all have been happy to be so adopted, abandoning their original family names in this way? How did their natural families react – or were they all simply abandoned as babies or with mothers who were wholly incapable of caring for them? In any event, they seem to have been happy and contented at St Hugh's, and to their signatures are added those of other boys who, while not Norman Potter's adopted sons, were resident at the Home and wanted to be associated with the statement being made:

> I state that I am the adopted son of Mr and Mrs Norman Potter and that neither before nor after my adoption have either my adopted father or mother on any occasion acted towards me in any immodest or wrong way and that they have not been guilty of any immodest act whatever with me. I make this statement of my own free will and under no compulsion or persuasion whatever.

The signatories are Sydney, Maurice, Gerard, Antony, Victor, Gordon, Oswald, Albert, Harold, Leonard, Basil, Eric, Paul, Gregory and H. F. Potter, together with Reginald and Ernest Hunt, C. Buller, and George and Robert Cole. This makes a total of fifteen adopted sons – and there must have been more because, as we have seen, there were others who were already away from home and serving in the Army. By any standards, making financial provision for all these boys on a long-term basis must have involved an enormous commitment, and represents an extraordinary human and financial involvement. It is impossible not to speculate on what happened to these young men. Some probably died in the slaughter of the First World War, but perhaps others went on to live to full age and marry and have families. Are there any descendants who can shed any light on this strange tale from 1914 and its aftermath?

The aftermath was, for Potter himself, nothing less than a tragedy that endured to his death. Stranded in Switzerland, cut off from his adopted sons, his reputation in ruins, he had to struggle to look after himself and his new young wife. The evidence against him does not appear to have been strong enough to warrant a legal prosecution, so perhaps it was nothing more than a mischievous or malicious boy telling an untruth, or, possibly, relating a half-believed fantasy. Can it indeed have been the case that this man, whose generosity and kindness produced so much good, had nevertheless struggled against dark and evil temptations and even given in to them?

On balance, Potter emerges as innocent: it seems unlikely that not one boy or young man emerged to corroborate the allegations made against him, and indeed all seem to have been genuinely astonished that such allegations could have been made at all.

Mr and Mrs Potter continued to live in Switzerland for many years. A letter from him to the Bishop, dated 1927, survives and reveals his anguish and sense of abandonment. He seems in fact to have left the Church for a time. He and his wife eventually opened their Swiss home as a holiday centre for boys from English public schools, and the ones listed on the brochure include several of the most famous schools but no Catholic ones.

His attempts to return home and see some of his boys again failed, and on a visit in 1920 he was banned from entering St Hugh's. He eventually died in 1934 and by this time he was reconciled to the Church – a letter from his wife in the diocesan archives described his receiving the Last Rites with great humility and devotion and on his death he was given an impressive funeral at St George's Cathedral, Southwark.

Was he the innocent victim of an appalling lie by a boy

whom he had befriended and was trying to help? We will simply never know – but the story is a haunting one.

Meanwhile, what had happened to St Hugh's? The diocesan authorities moved swiftly. By the middle of 1915 an entirely new St Hugh's Society had been established and had taken over the Home and, it seems, all the funds associated with it. Presumably the boys who were living there simply carried on as before, but without their father and under the care of new staff.

A booklet produced and circulated in mid-1915 for this new St Hugh's eerily creates a whole new version of the charity and simply writes out Potter and all his works as though they had never existed. There is reference to various properties in Clapham 'four freehold properties and one leasehold which had been acquired by public subscription and by the gift of a benefactor' and also 'a leasehold property at Clapham of which the house is let and the grounds are used as a football field, a part being let off to a Tennis Club.' References to 'St Joseph's' and to the 'St Crispin's Boot Shop' have vanished: it seems that all of these projects were simply handed over to others. It is announced that St Hugh's is a charity which aims to care for middle-class boys for whom a standard orphanage is unsuitable and who require residential care because one or both parents are dead or unable to look after them adequately. It takes some reading between the lines to establish that in fact these boys must include those who were already resident at St Hugh's when the scandal broke and Mr Potter had to leave. There is a reference, with some evident pride, to the fact that all of the former residents now of military age are serving with the Forces.

The emphasis, however, is on the future and the booklet gives details of plans to organize long-term assistance for boys from middle-class families who need a Catholic education and are in danger of being put into the care of non-Catholic friends or relations because of family poverty.

St Hugh's continued with this work throughout the

26

inter-war years and into the 1950s and 60s – it survived into the 1970s and was finally converted into a bursary fund enabling poorer boys to attend a major Catholic public school, Downside: this bursary continues to this day.

The other boys' homes initiated by Mr Potter all came under the care of the Southwark Diocese. One of them, St Joseph's, a home for working boys, was to be, as we will see, the scene of a wartime tragedy in Clapham Park which is still remembered.

The First World War, which involved the boys from Mr Potter's various homes, and many more local boys, brought many changes in its wake to Clapham Park. During the war, families grieved as sons, husbands and fathers were killed. Life became grim as food was rationed, news was bleak, and the vision of a bright new peaceful post-war world seemed unlikely.

One consequence of the war was that the Catholic church emerged as having a message of hope and realism to offer in a time of confusion and tragedy, and the 1920s and 30s were to see, everywhere in England, a thriving Catholic parish life. These years were to be a time of rapid growth for the Catholic community of Clapham Park, and to establish the parish as a strong entity.

La Retraite School was now a flourishing part of local life. It was both a boarding and day school. One family who joined the school shortly before the First World War were to have a long connection with both the school and the parish, stretching over three generations. Young Doris Hansen, her sister Yvonne, and their brother Leslie went to live at the school after their father's business failed and their mother (stage name Grace Wicksteed) had to return to work as an actress travelling around Britain with various plays and was thus unable to provide a permanent home. The three children seem to have been happy at the school, and their mother also arranged for them to travel with the nuns to Burnham in Somerset during the War

27

when Zeppelin raids posed a threat to Londoners. Later Doris herself became a nun, as Sister St Teresa, and after studying at London's Bedford College where she obtained a diploma, she became a teacher at La Retraite and went on to be headmistress. Yvonne married and settled locally, living in a flat in one of the big houses in Thornton Road in the 1920s – in due course her daughter, Joan Hitchings, became a pupil at La Retraite, and the family worshipped at St Bede's, where Joan made her first Holy Communion. (The family link is still kept up – Joan's daughter, Mrs Yvonne Windsor, is today, in 2002, a regular Mass attender at St Bede's.)

In 1921 Fr Francis Day came to live at St Bede's. His main work was as chaplain to Brixton Prison, for which he was paid an official Government salary. He gave a good part of this to the parish in payment for his food and lodging, and this was a great help in paying off the substantial debt on the church. Although he did some work in the parish, his work at the prison – and also at La Retraite Convent where he said Mass each Sunday – meant that Dr Hooley also had to have some extra help from a Salesian priest from Clapham College who came over on Sunday mornings to say the final Mass of the day (there were no evening Masses at that time).

A parishioner remembers:

My mother's family came to St Bede's in 1918. She met my father, who had just come out of the army, through mutual friends in the parish. They belonged to a Tennis Club at St Bede's where there was a court in the garden.

They were married by Father Thomas Hooley in 1922, the altar boy at their wedding being the young Andrew Beck who later became a Bishop ...

The Beck family, who lived in Weir Road, Clapham Park, were well known in the parish. George Andrew Beck and his brother John were both keen altar servers and both became priests. Their sister became a nun at La Retraite

28

as Sister Mary Andrew. Sadly, John died just three months after his ordination. George Andrew went on to become a well-known priest and eventually Archbishop of Liverpool.

In 1923 in his notes following his official Visitation to the parish, Bishop Amigo wrote to Dr Hooley:

> You have done exceedingly well in your efforts to pay off the debt and I congratulate you most heartily. I shall be very pleased to erect St Bede's into a parish, now that you hope to pay off the debt in a year. You will have the document in a few days. I am glad that your Church is open all day and that the number of Communions is increasing ... You had a very good congregation for my visitation.

The Bishop had attended the church to confirm a number of children even though he was suffering from a bad cold and had difficulty preaching. The school, which he described as 'excellent' had 43 pupils and there was now also a convent school for older girls with 208 pupils, of whom about half were non-Catholics.

Dr Hooley's deep friendship with Cardinal Bourne must have been something of a trial to Archbishop Amigo throughout the 1920s. Bourne visited Dr Hooley, as we have seen, every week, to go to confession and to have lunch. The children at the school used to look out of the classroom windows to note his arrival – he was a well-known figure as he turned up each week at Clapham Park.

In 1927 Dr Hooley published a book *A Seminary in the Making*, a history of St John's Seminary, Wonersh. It carried a foreword by Cardinal Bourne, and most of the book was essentially a tribute to Bourne's work in founding the seminary, with long extracts from his sermons and speeches. In effect, the book was a declaration of loyalty to Cardinal Bourne, just at the time when the Cardinal was continuing his efforts to take over Southwark Diocese and merge it with his own at Westminster. Dr Hooley

29

had become known in the Diocese of Southwark as a 'Bourne-ite' and in this capacity was inevitably something of a thorn in the side of Archbishop Amigo.

Clapham Park was growing rapidly as a suburb. Commuting was now a way of life, with the Tube established as a speedy way of getting into central London, and buses rumbling along the main roads. The large mansions of the early nineteenth century had already begun to disappear and now the streets of small Victorian terraced houses were joined by further developments as pebble-dashed semi-detached homes were built nearby.

The First World War had brought big social changes too. Women were going out to work in offices and shops. Fewer and fewer homes were likely to have cooks or maids, and girls were beginning to feel more independent as they worked in industry or commerce. They wore shorter skirts and, along with their brothers, took part in the now fashionable sports and hiking trips. Scouts and Guide groups began to flourish. New leisure activities, such as going to the cinema and listening to the wireless (radio) were popular and created new trends in music and speech.

Catholic life reflected these changes. There was a growing social side to parish life as the Catholic population in South London grew. There was a strong community feeling at St Bede's. The people were proud of their little church and of being Catholics. The building began to feel cramped as the numbers at Mass steadily increased.

The church at that time was considerably smaller than the one we see today. There was no sacristy or Lady chapel and the building was only the length of the present nave. Behind it – on land now occupied by the sanctuary, Lady chapel, etc. – was a garden which also extended over much of the land now taken up by the present St Bede's School.

A parishioner has childhood memories of what it was like:

The confessional was at the back of the church, mysteriously shrouded in black velvet curtains. Where the hymnbook cupboard is now was a door and a flight of steps up to the Presbytery and Parish Room. This room was L-shaped. The Billiard Room was where the kitchen is today. The present Dining Room was the main part of the Parish Room with double doors leading into the room which is now Father's office. I believe it was in there that the vestments etc were kept. We used to help the Sacristan clean the candlesticks and as I remember we were in the Parish Room ...

The priests' kitchen was in the basement – terribly dark and gloomy, but cheered up to some extent by the Housekeeper's many birds in cages along the wall. She used to chatter all the time to the birds and was most kind to us. Before our Religious Knowledge exams she used to hear our Catechism while we sat in her tiny drawing room which was where the basement kitchen now is.

By the late 1920s the church was evidently much too small for the congregation and an extension was necessary. In January 1927 a Church Extension Fund was started. This meant increased efforts at fund-raising, and the annual Garden Parties became a major feature of parish life. These were always held at the beginning of July:

> These parties were held on two Saturdays and also the Wednesday in between. They were quite special events in the neighbourhood – social occasions as well as for money-raising.
>
> One of the attractions of the garden party was a wooden shute which had to be highly polished to make it slippery. It had wooden sides to stop us from falling off. However as we sped down our legs would be grazed on these until we had horrid raw patches on them and had to stop. One of the parishioners worked a kitchen garden beyond the shute and on it he kept bees so that was another hazard of the day!
>
> There was an awning drawn up over the lawn where

there were refreshments. There was talk of carving large hams in the evening but we were not allowed to stay up for that and had to go when the lights came on for the evening. I do remember the ladies turning up in their party frocks. There were stage shows as well with singing and dancing – and some horrific talent competitions!

Confirmation records in the parish register for the 1920s show good numbers of boys and girls being confirmed. In those days, it was usual to have just one person being sponsor for all the girls and one for all the boys – a different procedure from today, when boys and girls are invited to choose their own sponsor, usually a relation or family friend. The sponsor for the girls for the Confirmations of 1921, 1923, 1925 and through to 1927 and 1929 was Josephine O'Brien, who was probably the parish catechist during those years.

Throughout the l920s and 30s Fr Hooley was anxious to extend the parish school, which was now much too small for its occupants. He was in constant negotiations with the education authorities about this. The school was a popular one, and Sister St Edith was a well known figure in the parish – 'a feisty little nun' as one parishioner remembers her. Fr Hooley took an interest in all the pupils: 'He could not bear to see anyone left out or not get a prize so he instituted a prize for anyone who "tried to improve"!' The school building was also used for parish plays – one year a magnificent production of Shakespeare's *Hamlet* in full costume – and for the parish Garden Parties it was transformed into a 'haunted house' to thrill young visitors.

Among the papers still at St Bede's are the Minutes of the 1931 Garden Party Committee of the Guild of the Blessed Sacrament. Present were the Brother Warden, and Brothers Alexander, Davis, Greenstock, Saunders and Cowan. (Interestingly, Brother Greenstock later went on to become Fr Greenstock, and was appointed Rector of the

English College at Valladolid in Spain.) The committee had evidently been established to look at the new arrangements necessary following the alterations to the garden layout with the building of a church extension. Brother Cowan, appointed as secretary, 'stated that Fr Hooley had places at his disposal the existing records of the Garden Party since its beginnings in 1905 and from these he had been able to arrange in handy form annual summaries which he trusted would be of assistance to the Cttee'. All sorts of details were then discussed, culminating in a lengthy report produced for the parish. Admission to the 1932 Garden Party would be 6d. for adults and 3d. for children (amounts approximating to 2 pence and 1 penny in today's currency). A detailed plan of the new garden area was to be created, and stalls on the day would be arranged 'in street form so that one might bring trade to its neighbours and strangers could discover prices without looking conspicuous at isolated stalls.' An interesting comment on how times have changed is the attention paid to cigarettes: among the suggested games and amusements on offer was a 'banker for cigarettes'. It was noted that there was always a high demand for cigarettes at the Garden Party and 'it was thought that this game which is said to be very fast might be run at intervals. Sweets and cigarettes were the original prizes mentioned but sweets were cut out as the game would interfere with the sweet stall. The disposal of cigarettes in this way was considered more profitable than straight sales under licence.' Other games suggested were skee-ball, quoits, skittles, and a rifle range. There was also a 'horse with a rotary body' which was popular at the Clapham College Garden party – but there was some concern about this because 'although popular it was dangerous for children unless thick mats were provided to break falls', and it was also considered unsuitable for ladies. A leading figure at the Garden Party was a Miss O'Brien, who seems to have been in charge of ticket sales, and for whom a brand new stall was planned following the committee's deliberations.

Another feature of parish life in the 1930s was the 'outdoor collection' – so named, presumably, to distinguish it from the 'indoor collection' held at Mass on Sundays. It was launched by Fr Hooley and largely manned by members of the Guild of the Blessed Sacrament, a men's group which played a central part in parish life. Families in the parish pledged to contribute a certain (usually modest) sum to the parish each week, and the collectors would go round each week to collect it – each man having specific roads which were his responsibility. There were about thirty such 'collection rounds' so the team of men involved was substantial. Each month the exact amount collected for the school fund would be announced in church – right down to the last halfpenny. These were the days before 'Gift aid' schemes and before most ordinary families used systems such as standing orders on a bank account.

The Guild of the Blessed Sacrament was an international Catholic organization for men, formed as its name implies to foster devotion to the Blessed Sacrament. Specifically, it existed to encourage men to receive Holy Communion on a regular basis. In the 1920s and 30s, the rule of the Church was that anyone receiving Holy Communion must fast from midnight. In practice, this meant that only those attending an early morning Mass were likely to go to Holy Communion. To get to Mass at 8 a.m. regularly on Sundays is quite a challenge for most busy working people. It was easy, therefore, to slip into the habit of attending a later Mass – having already breakfasted – and thus not to receive Holy Communion at all. The Guild thus held a monthly 'Corporate Communion' – an 8 a.m. Mass which all would agree to attend and receive Holy Communion together. Members of the Guild would fill the first five or six pews in the church – and many would attend St Bede's again later in the day for the an evening Rosary procession followed by Benediction. These men formed the core of the parish's active workers, and could be relied upon to take up any task that was needed.

St Bede's Clapham Park, in the early 1930s. Note the white arch which then marked the entrance from Thornton Road and was local people's main memory of the church.

St. BEDE'S,

Thornton Road, Clapham Park, s.w.

APPEAL FOR THE NEW INFANTS' SCHOOL.

The Mission of St. Bede was founded on Sept. 8th, 1903, the services being held in rooms at Hyde House.

On Nov. 4th, 1905, the foundation stone of the New Church was laid, and on April 27th, 1906, the Church was formally opened by His Lordship the Bishop of Southwark.

The steady increase in the number of Catholics in the district (the average attendance at Mass on Sunday is over 300) has made the provision of an Elementary School for the younger children an absolute necessity, and this has been made possible through the kindness of the Nuns of the La Retraite Convent, who have undertaken to do the teaching gratuitously.

The Hall beside the Presbytery has been converted into an excellent school-room, suitable for about 40 children, with cloak-room and everything necessary for an up-to-date schoolroom. These alterations have been carried out at a cost of £33 10s., and the necessary equipment has cost nearly £20. So the New School has involved an initial expenditure of £50. To meet this, a sum of £28 has been raised, of which amount only £6 10s. has come from the congregation. A year ago the capital debt on the Church amounted to £2,330 11s. 6d. This amount has been reduced by £65, and the year's interest, which came to nearly £94, has been paid. This heavy debt should prevent any further obligations being undertaken, but the imminent danger to the Faith of a number of children, through attending Non-Catholic Schools on account of there being no Catholic School in the district, is a sufficient reason to ask the Congregation to make a special effort to start the New School.

I earnestly ask all who can to help in this matter by contributing something towards the £22 yet required.

Members of the Congregation are invited to visit the School and judge for themselves of the value and necessity of the work being done.

THOMAS HOOLEY.

September 1910.

An early appeal for funds for a parish school, 1910.

SAINT HUGH'S ACCOUNTS
For the Year Ending 1909

In answer to your petition, we heartily impart the apostolic blessing upon our beloved son, Norman F. Potter, his family, and all his works.—PIUS X, PP·

Dear Mr Norman Potter,

I HAVE laid before the Ho'y Father your request for a special blessing on the work which you have undertaken, at the request of the Archbishop of Westminster, for the Catholic cripples in the South of England.

At the same time, I acquainted His Holiness with the information you gave me regarding the progress of the work during the past two years, and the necessity of further expansion in order to meet the demands you receive, and to prevent many poor children, already so greatly afflicted, from being exposed to the further calamity of losing their faith.

His Holiness was much gratified to learn how much has already been done, by you and your co-operators in this excellent work of charity, to lessen, as far as possible, the disabilities by which these children suffer and to provide for them a suitable home. He trusts that your desire to be enabled to receive every child who should find a place in a Catholic Home, may be fulfilled. And, praying God to bestow abundant graces on the work, His Holiness affectionately imparts to you, to the cripples, and to all who join with you in befriending them, the Apostolic Benediction.

I am, Yours devotedly in C. J.

R. CARD. MERRY DEL VAL

ST HUGH'S, THORNTON RD, CLAPHAM PARK, LONDON, S.W.

Front page of the annual accounts for Mr Norman Potter's homes for orphans and handicapped boys.

FRANCISCVS

TITVLI SANCTAE PVDENTIANAE
SANCTAE ROMANAE ECCLESIAE

PRESBYTER CARDINALIS BOVRNE

DEI ET APOSTOLICAE SEDIS GRATIA

ARCHIEPISCOPVS
WESTMONASTERIENSIS.

COETVS EPISCOPALIS TOTIVS ANGLIAE
ET CAMBRIAE PRAESES PERPETVVS.

Per has praesentes fidem facimus ac testamur

Nos die 30ª Junii, 1930, facultate S. R. E.

Cardinalibus concessa, V I A M   C R U C I S

in Ecclesia Sancti Bedae Venerabilis   apud

Clapham Park erexisse ac benedixisse.

Datum Westmonasterii, die 2ª Julii, 1932.

1. Card. Bourne
Archiepus Westmonasterien.

De mandato Emi et Rmi Dni mei Cardinalis Archiepiscopi.

E. Mourgh Bernard.

Formal permission from Cardinal Bourne for the erection of the Stations of
the Cross, 1932.

Sister St Teresa (Doris Hansen), headmistress of La Retraite, in the heavy
veil and habit which the Sisters wore until the 1960s.

Dr Hooley in his study in the late 1940s.

Cardinal Bourne (right) with Dr Hooley, long-time parish priest of St Bede's.

Dr Hooley's Golden Jubilee ceremony at La Retraite School Hall, 1949. Archbishop Beck of Liverpool, who had grown up in Clapham Park, was a special guest.

Parish summer fete, with many of the children in fancy dress. The date is uncertain – probably 1954.

Fr O'Connor's Silver Jubilee, 1959. Mr Walter Keenan makes the presentation at a parish social.

First Communion, 1959 or 1960.

The outside altar for Corpus Christi, created in flowers by Michael Atkinson, late 1960s.

First Communion – with the UCM providing a feast, 1970.

Fr Hugh Thwaites SJ, Fr Michael Creech CssR, Fr Christopher Basden, 1995 – and the usual solemn reverence among the altar servers!

Altar servers on an outing, 1995. The medals around their necks indicate membership of the Guild of St Stephen.

Parish dinner, 1995. David and Veronica Pierson with Kathy Mirza and Fr Michael Creech, CSSR.

Parishioner Margaret Howard, a well-known radio broadcaster with the BBC and Classic FM, opens the parish bazaar, 1998.

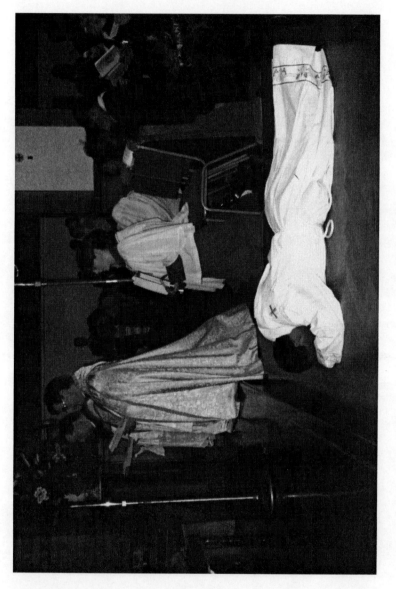

An ordination at St Bede's: Fr Philip de Freitas, prostrate before the altar at his ordination, 1997.

Archbishop Michael Bowen visited the parish in 1998 to greet the Spanish sisters who were moving into the convent vacated by the Sisters of La Retraite.

First Communion group, 1990s. Catechists join the clergy and children for a commemorative picture. The boys wear red sashes across their shoulders – a tradition dating back to the days of the Guild of the Blessed Sacrament almost a century earlier.
Front row, left to right: Mr Keith de Cruz (Head), Angela Murphy, Dom Andrew, Fr Christopher, Mary Harding, Sister Augustina.

Fr Ronald Salmon 1967–1981

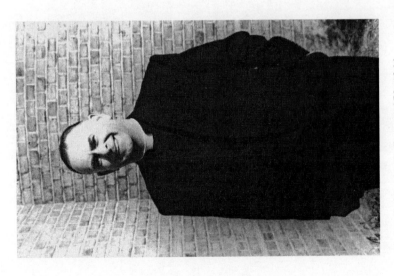

Fr Joseph Sullivan 1959–1966

Playing around with hats! Fr Leopoldo (Mexico), Fr Richard Moth (England, wearing a boater!), Fr William Dinan (Ireland, wearing a riding hat!).

Mgr Leo White and parish Cub Scouts celebrating his birthday, St Patrick's Nite, 2000.

Parish Scouts on an outing to Disney World, Paris, 2000, with Fr Adam Pergol.

Three head teachers in the Millenium Year, 2000: Mrs Maureen Howie (La Retraite), Mr Keith de Cruz (St Bernadette's), Mrs Ann Henshaw (St Bede's).

The Handmaids of Mary at the former La Retraite Convent. Mother Lourdes Susaeta Superior, second from the left on the front row. They arrived at Easter 1998.

Confirmation, February 2001 with Bishop Charles Henderson.

Catalina and Catherine Snowdon with the Sosa musicians from Latin America.

St Bede's Afro-Carribbean Association with Fr Valentine Awoyemi, 2001.

The parish clergy, Easter 2002. Left to right (back): Fr Armand de Malleray FSSP, Fr Casimir Adjoe of Ghana, Fr Andrew Southwell, OSB. Front (sitting): Mgr Leo White, Fr Christopher Basden, parish priest.

A leaflet dating from the 1930s, still in the archives at St Bede's, invites local men to join:

The Brothers of the Guild of the Blessed Sacrament desire to interest you in its work and purpose, and hope to have the pleasure of enrolling you as a member.

The Guild imposes only two duties – attendance together at Holy Communion on the first Sunday in each month, and at the Procession and Benediction together on the same day. But the Guild is not merely a matter of devotional observance; it has a week-day interest and an appeal of a social and intellectual kind. It affords an invaluable means of interesting laymen of all classes in the subjects of the day and giving them an opportunity to exchange opinion. What is more important, it opens their eyes to the fact that on many passing affairs there is a Catholic aspect to be considered.

Considering the size of the parish, the Guild has every reason, so far, to be satisfied with its success. But it is felt that, with an increased membership, its usefulness might be extended and its social evenings made more frequent.

Information regarding the Guild may be obtained from Father HOOLEY or any member of the Guild, and a warm invitation is offered to all new-comers to the parish.

Fund-raising was evidently a major part of Catholic parish life in the 1930s, and at St Bede's this was especially the case, as both the school and the extending of the church meant considerable expenditure of money. Clapham Park was not a well-to-do area, and these years between the two World Wars were not prosperous times for most ordinary families, so the burden on them all must have been considerable.

The church extension was opened in 1932, with a special High Mass celebrated by Fr John Beck on Whit Monday.

This young priest had been born in the parish and had been an altar server at St Bede's for many years. It was a matter for considerable parish pride when he went on to become a priest, and he had celebrated his first Mass in the parish back in 1928. Now, at this special event, there were to be other distinguished visitors. Assisting him at the Mass were Fr Hanlon, who was rector when the church was built, and Fr Fitzgibbon, under whose pastoral care the parish had begun back in 1903. But the most important guest was Cardinal Bourne, who preached the sermon. This was a major event in the history of St Bede's. What had begun as a small chapel in a house was now a thriving parish, and the church was making a considerable impact on the neighbourhood. The extension did not alter the fundamentally simple outlines of the church, but merely increased seating space by pushing out the chancel into what had been part of the rear garden and opening up more of the nave.

Fr Hooley's choice of Cardinal Bourne to be the special guest and preacher was definitely unusual in that it would have been more normal to have invited the local bishop. His decision to invite the Cardinal was obviously because Bourne was a longtime friend, but it evidently caused some (understandable!) tension with Archbishop Amigo. A note by Amigo in the Southwark diocesan archives, made in September 1933 on his official Visitation to the parish, says 'Church extension was opened by Cardinal Bourne on Whit Monday 1932 but I was not invited or told.' Meanwhile in the commemorative brochure published to mark the occasion (presumably written by Dr Hooley) the glory goes to Cardinal Bourne: 'The Cardinal will assist at the Mass and preach, thus crowning the completion of the work, the beginning of which was the final act of his own episcopate in Southwark.'

At the same time as the new church extension was formally opened, a new set of Stations of the Cross was evidently erected, as a document in the parish records dated 2 July 1932 notes the erection and blessing of a

'VIAM CRUCIS in Ecclesia Sancti Bedae Venerabilis apud Clapham Park.' All Church documents were written in Latin in those days. The blessing came from 'Franciscus Presbyter Cardinalis Bourne, Dei et Apostolicae Sedis Gratia ARCHIPIEPISCOPUS WESTMONASERIENSIS' rather than 'Petrus EPISCUPUS SOUTHWARCENSIS', so even in the parish documents there is evidence of the tension between Cardinal Bourne and Archbishop Amigo over the matter of Episcopal authority at Clapham Park.

The church, then as now, was approached by a path leading off from Thornton Road, through a small garden area. Where today's lychgate stands at the entrance to this path was a simpler white arch topped by a cross.

Parish activities tended to be more formal than would be the norm today, with separate organizations for men and women. People also tended to address one another more formally – even those who had been friends and neighbours for years would still call one another 'Mr' or 'Mrs' so-and-so. Children invariably addressed all adults formally and would not dream of using an adult's Christian name. Although everyday dress was more informal than it had been in the 1900s, all men would certainly wear a jacket and tie to attend Mass, and women wore hats. No woman would have considered the possibility of attending church in trousers, or even in an everyday skirt and jumper: it was usual to have a 'Sunday dress'. Silence was invariably kept in church, with all communication carried out in whispers or very low voices. Mass was of course said in Latin, the priest using a low voice, and most people brought their own Prayer Books with them and followed silently. Boys who became altar servers learned the Latin responses by heart.

The spiritual life of the parish was vigorous, and numbers attending Mass continued to rise steadily throughout the 1920s and 30s. A sample of the approach taken can be seen in a handbill for a parish mission held in the Spring of 1934. Starting with a Solemn Opening at the 11 a.m. Mass on 11 March, it included Mass at 7.30 and

9.30 a.m. each day, with a Meditation on the Passion of Christ after the 11 a.m. Mass. Each evening there was recitation of the Rosary, a Mission Service, and Benediction at 8 p.m. There were special Children's Mission services on the Sunday, Monday, and Tuesday at 5.30 p.m. The Mission was preached by a Passionist priest, Fr Benignus, and the whole aim was to encourage people to think seriously about their eternal salvation. The handbill, after quoting the New Testament 'What doth it profit a man, if he gain the whole world, and suffer the loss of his own soul', gave a solemn reminder: 'Remember (1) That the salvation of our own soul is the ONE thing necessary; (2) That the time is short; (3) That this Mission may determine YOUR eternity'.

That same year, 1934, marked the Silver Jubilee of Fr Hooley's time at St Bede's – he had been parish priest for twenty-five years. On 22 January a Mr Hibberd wrote on behalf of the parish to the Bishop:

> My Lord
> As you are probably aware, on the 15th August Father Hooley celebrated his Silver Jubilee as Rector of St Bede's.
>
> With his usual modesty, he deprecates the idea of a personal gift to mark this event and it has therefore been decided that a 'mile of pennies' be collected as a token of the parish's esteem, the proceeds to go towards reducing the debt caused through the Church Extension. May I on behalf of the sub-committee appointed to carry out the work involved, respectfully ask your approval, together with a blessing on the project in question.

Approval was given, and the scheme went ahead.

That same year some further structural alterations had to be made to the church. A crack had appeared in the arch surrounding the entrance to the chancel. A surveyor's report indicated that the problem lay in subsidence: 'Clay subsoil affected by two successive and abnormally dry Summers'. It was necessary to do some repair work: 'Prepare centring piece for Arch as may be necessary and shore up same. Cut out all defective and damaged brickwork to arch and walls and make good same. Supply and fix extra strong [illegible] rod at back of Chancel Arch to extend the full width of Gable and anchored round and into the main return walls of building.' No wonder the most useful gift the parishioners could make to Fr Hooley was cash for the church funds!

The life of the parish was very much bound up with that of La Retraite Convent, where many of the girls went to school, and with the little St Bede's School. The nuns at La Retraite at that time dressed in distinctive voluminous habits that reached to the ground, with heavy veils framing their faces. They made their own mark on the neighbourhood and by the middle 1930s were an established presence, much respected locally – although 100 years earlier most ordinary residents of Clapham and the surrounding suburbs would never have seen a nun and would have regarded them, if they thought about them at all, as weird and foreign and rather sinister.

Although the little school at St Bede's was poorly equipped by modern standards, it was popular with the parish families and boasted its own attractions – included two full-sized rocking horses which the children loved!

During these inter-war years, the whole parish grew and thrived. On the outbreak of the Second World War in 1939, St Bede's was a strong Catholic community. There were all sorts of groups, including a branch of the Guild of St Agnes for Girls, which was formally inaugurated in May 1939. Founding a Guild of this sort required permission from the Bishop, and the letter duly came from Archbishop's House at Southwark, signed by the Archbishop's Secretary, Fr Cyril Cowderoy, himself a future Archbishop.

There were other groups, too. A parishioner recalls:

Just before the war my sister-in-law started the first Youth Club at St Bede's and also the first Bazaar. She had only just left school at La Retraite and wanted all the young people in the parish to join. It was very successful. They organised all sorts of events and went hiking in the country. The inside of the presbytery needed brightening up so they worked hard with the curate Father Terence Quinlan to paint the walls.

Inevitably, the war meant that many of the young men of the parish were to go away, to serve in the Army, Navy, or Air Force. Some families moved away, too, to get away from the dangers of air raids. The blackout regulations each night meant that all the roads were plunged into darkness – no street lights, no beam of light emerging from behind the thick dark curtains that were now compulsory in every window of every house. This made for difficulties in running any evening event, and all kinds of parish activities had to be abandoned or altered to fit into wartime conditions.

La Retraite School was evacuated to Hampshire, and Clapham College to East Grinstead. Some children did return to Clapham later in the war when the danger from bombing seemed to be over. Later, in peacetime, the Sisters at La Retraite erected a statue of St Joan in thanksgiving for the fact that none of the children evacuated with the schools had been killed by bombing during the war.

A parishioner remembers, 'Daily Mass went on at St Bede's and there was also a Holy Hour every Friday evening. I only remember Fr Hooley stopping a service once when a bomb landed particularly close. No one, luckily, was injured, and we all resumed our places.'

Some of the young men who had been in the parish youth club and then left to join the Services never came back – they were killed on active service. There were deaths nearer to home during these war years, too. In the summer of 1940, as a preparation for the planned invasion of Britain, the German Air Force attacked London in what came to be known as the Blitz. Fierce bombing raids continued through the September and October of that year. On the night of 16 October, a raider dropped a stick of bombs across Balham and Clapham Park. One fell on Balham Tube station, which was packed to capacity at the time. Many people had thought that it was safe to shelter underground in the stations – but this was not always so, and the scene at Balham was one of carnage. The station is not far below the surface of the ground and the bomb burst a water main which added to the horror. A total of sixty-four people were killed and a plaque in the station now records the tragedy.

Another bomb fell almost immediately opposite St Bede's, in a direct hit on number 129 Kings Avenue which was, of course, St Joseph's, a home for Catholic boys originally founded by Mr Norman Potter. Four young boys were killed – Peter Murphy, aged ten, Octobris Augustine Murphy, aged nine, Dennis Edwards aged sixteen, and Reginald Bestam, aged eighteen. Also killed were Mr and Mrs Murphy, who ran the home (Peter and Octobris were their sons), another helper Helena O'Flaherty, aged thirty, and a priest Fr Richard Barry. Fr Barry was only thirty-two and had been a popular and hard-working priest who played a big part in the lives of children being cared for by the Diocese of Southwark.

The dead were brought into the church for burial, and an eyewitness remembers, 'The sight of so many coffins in St Bede's is something those who were there will never forget.' Fr Barry's body was buried at Brockley and the others at Magdalen Road, Wandsworth. This tragedy was perhaps the saddest single event in the history of St Bede's and is the event that most parishioners who lived in Clapham Park during the Second World War remember.

In 1942 Archbishop Amigo, now aged eighty, made a formal Visitation to the parish and his subsequent letter to the parish priest makes solemn reading, giving some flavour of wartime life:

I am sorry that the Visitation was delayed and that I had to make it on a weekday and at a time when the 'black out' made it difficult for the congregation, but you had a good number present ... It is discouraging to see so many children evacuated and the congregation so diminished. It is doubtful whether four Masses are necessary on Sundays ... I wish those who remain in the parish could come better to weekday Mass and to your evening service especially in Lent in order to obtain God's blessing on this Country.

You had a terrible catastrophe in the destruction of the Boys' Home with nine deaths. Other bombs have fallen in the district. Fortunately you have not suffered as much as some other parishes ...

In his sermon notes for his visit, which still survive in the diocesan archives, Archbishop Amigo wrote:

all to pray earnestly; we are engaged in a terrible war and not winning; we must make ourselves worthy of victory; all turn to God for help; King has asked for days of prayer and we Catholics have responded, but many don't know God and don't pray; show the examples as evacuated children have done in some parts and produced great impression.

Fr Quinlan, the curate in the parish, had spent many nights on 'fire watch' duty: sometimes incendiary bombs were dropped and it was possible to extinguish them before the fire took hold and caused damage. 'Fire watching' was a big part of wartime life for people in Britain's cities. Later Fr Quinlan was called up for Army service as a chaplain, and he served with the Commandos during the 1944 invasion of Europe via Normandy, which saw such bitter fighting and finally brought the war to a close.

An official body, the War Damage Commission – which had its London regional Office at 55, Eden Street, Kingston-upon-Thames – paid for repairs following bomb attacks. Obviously all major rebuilding would have to wait until the end of the war, but in September 1942 St Bede's received the sum of £110. 19s. 7d., which was paid direct to the builders, Hussey Bros, at 60, Queensway, Bayswater. This was the result of much form-filling by Fr Hooley, following repair work carried out in December 1940. The actual work was done by a local firm, Crabb and Son 'Builders, Decorators and Funeral Directors', at Tulse Hill. It mostly consisted of minor repairs to the windows, fixing slates to the roof where they had slipped off, and work on the damaged porch. There were also broken windows in the presbytery and damage to some outbuildings including one described as the Old Harness Room, where some boarding had been damaged by fire.

The war did bring happier events, too: one soldier who was serving in the area with a bomb disposal unit, stationed in Atkins Road, joined the choir at St Bede's where he was a great asset as he had a fine tenor voice and a great knowledge of plainchant. He later married one of the girls in the parish and settled locally.

When the war ended and people started to trickle back to Clapham Park, there was a great sense of relief that normal life could now be resumed. The youth club was re-started, but each meeting now included prayers for all the boys who had been members and who had later died in the war – these prayers continued for many years.

A major preoccupation for the parish as soon as the war ended was the provision of a parish school. With peace not even yet certain – the fighting with Japan was still continuing – Fr Hooley was writing in March 1945 to the Ministry of Education in Belgrave Square:

Re: proposed RC JM School Thornton Rd etc. I beg to remind you that negotiations for the building of the above school had reached their penultimate stage immediately prior to the outbreak of War: notices had been published, the Board had approved in principle; and it merely remained to discuss the actual building plans. It is

43

fair to state that but for the outbreak of hostilities, the school would long since have been functioning.

At the moment, because the school could not be built, the children who would have been attending it are forced to go elsewhere: those whose parents can afford fees, are sent to La Retraite Convent school. Those whose parents are less fortunately placed either attend my private elementary school – if aged 5–8 – or are obliged to travel long distances to existing Catholic schools or – where that is not possible – to attend non-Catholic schools ...'

Thus began the campaign to get the St Bede's school project off the ground – which was to dominate the parish's fund-raising and other activities for the next few years.

Later Mgr Edward Mahoney, on behalf of the diocese, established with the Ministry of Education the scheme that was to be used for primary education in Clapham Park: 'It has now been agreed that the Girls School and the Infants will be accommodated on a site within the Convent and grounds ... The Nuns will have all the Infants (mixed) and Junior Girls, leaving only the Junior Boys which will be for 120 to 160 only.'

In 1947 a Parish Entertainments Committee was formed – clear evidence of the revival of parish life after the war years. The Minutes Book (wording and punctuation not edited) notes that:

Its object is to provide a little more Social Life in the Parish and especially to help in the enormous task which lies ahead, namely, the raising of funds for the new School. The Bazaar held last Christmas and the Bring and Buy Sale in the Summer were very successful. We are all pleased with such a good beginning. It is felt that in the future much bigger efforts must be made. To ensure the widest cooperation from the Parish it is necessary to have a representative Committee.

The Entertainments Committee consists of members from the different organisations of the Parish, with Father O'Driscoll as President, a preliminary meeting was held when it was decided to have two persons representing their particular organisation and who should be voted for, from their respective Councils.

The Committee met regularly, with Mr Cowie being elected Treasurer. Mr Keenan represented the St Vincent de Paul Society, Mrs Davies the Guild, Mrs Hoole and Mrs Cowie the Catholic Women's League, Miss Brinn and Mr Crotty the Club, and Miss Marshall and Miss Ritters the Children of Mary. From the minutes it is clear that Miss Marshall was kept busy, as it was her task to arrange for the printing of 500 circular letters about the Bazaar, which were distributed after all the Masses.

Funds raised seem small by today's standards. The first of a series of monthly Whist Drives netted £4.17s. 8½d., of which £2. 0s. 2½d. was required for expenses, leaving just £2. 0s. 2d. to be handed over to Fr Hooley for the school fund.

In 1949 Fr Hooley reached a major landmark in his life, about which the treasurer of the Committee wrote to members of the parish:

On April 30th 1949 Father Hooley celebrates his Golden Jubilee. Those of us who have had the privilege of knowing him for any period during his fifty years of priesthood cannot fail to have gained strength from his faith, courage and ready willingness to help, particularly in times of trouble.

Now comes our opportunity to show a little of that appreciation which is so difficult to express in words. It is proposed to make a suitable presentation to him next April and a Fund has been started for this purpose. A Committee, representative of all organisations in the parish, will be responsible for co-ordinating activities to this end ...

45

The letter went on to beg for secrecy: 'We want this to be a surprise, so please refrain from mentioning this matter to Fr Hooley until the appropriate time.' Ideas and suggestions for the form the presentation should make were welcomed.

The appeal was supported with great enthusiasm. People sent in their gifts by cheque and postal order. Many sent £5 – a large sum in those days. Among the gifts chosen were a set of Mass vestments, made at a convent in Effingham – these were laid out for view at a special committee meeting on 28 April where, the minutes record 'the Committee expressed unanimous satisfaction and grateful thanks to Miss Davis [who had arranged for this purchase]. The vestments should be presented with the cheque to Fr Hooley at the Presentation meeting. The Treasurer reported that the total of £342-6-6 had been reached.'

A special Apostolic Blessing was sent to Fr Hooley from Pope Pius XII and in passing it on, Bishop Amigo sent a warm note of friendship: 'I congratulate you most heartily on your Golden Jubilee. You have done great work for God in these 50 years. I join you in thanking God for all the many graces which He has bestowed upon you. May He spare you to the Diocese for a long time still ...' The note is written in something of a laboured scrawl and there is a touching PS: 'My eyesight is bad and I find it hard to read and write.'

In due course a great parish gathering was held on Sunday, 1 May 1949 at La Retraite Convent, followed by Benediction at St Bede's. Bishop Beck – from the local family which had produced two priests and a nun and who was to go on to become Archbishop of Liverpool – was the main speaker at the gathering and he was followed by Fr O'Driscoll, Fr Fitzgibbon, and various members of the parish. The parish was now large and thriving. For the Garden Fete in the summer of 1949, arrangements had to be made for refreshments for 250 children. The event grew steadily in size and included a dancing display, boxing matches, a talent competition and a big Parish Show which took place in the evening and was the climax of the day.

In fact, in the late 1940s and throughout the 1950s, Clapham Park and parish life at St Bede's continued very much as it had done before the war. Although there were bomb-sites that scarred the landscape, the pace of life itself was unchanged. These were the days when most families still did not have televisions, or own their own cars. Few mothers went out to work. Most people still dressed formally – jackets and ties for men most days, and as a matter of course best clothes for Mass on Sundays. People were beginning to use new words, such as 'teenager', but the whole pop culture of the 1960s, and the massive social revolution that took place at the end of that decade and the early years of the 1970s, was yet to come. Clapham Park itself still consisted mostly of large old houses, although by now many of them were divided into flats. The large blocks of Council flats were not built until the 1960s.

In 1949 Archbishop Amigo died, and was succeeded by Bishop Cyril Cowderoy. The last years of his episcopacy were spent partly in arranging for the rebuilding of St George's Cathedral, which had been virtually destroyed in a wartime bombing raid.

1950 was decreed by the Church to be a Holy Year, which entailed special ceremonies and celebrations. The Guild of the Blessed Sacrament was now going strongly again after the war years, and it now met annually with members of the Guild from other parts of the diocese for a special procession in the ruins of St George's Cathedral. A parishioner remembers that, after the various religious ceremonies, all the men would go off to nearby pubs: in those days these remained open only until 10 p.m. in the Southwark area, but those in Westminster, across the Thames, closed at 10.30 p.m. and so many would hurry over there for a final pint!

Another strong parish organization was the Children of Mary – already mentioned among the organizations

47

working together on the Entertainments Committee. The members were the young unmarried girls of the parish and they met regularly to pray the Rosary and attend Benediction together. When a girl got married, she left the group – and was always presented with a statue of Mary for her future home.

There was also the Legion of Mary, a quite different group concerned with Catholic action in many fields (still active across Britain) This met weekly. Its members – who addressed each other as Sister this or Brother that at meetings – went visiting the various houses in the parish, distributing material about the Church, and encouraging lapsed Catholics to return to the faith. In the early 1950s the leader was Sister Kearney, assisted by Sister Watt, with Sister Fitzgerald as Secretary.

St Bede's also had a branch of the St Vincent de Paul Society, under Mr Keenan and Mr Cowie, which worked to raise funds and distribute them to the poor and needy.

Something of the atmosphere of parish life in the 1950s is discernible from the Year Book for 1953–54. Over fifty baptisms are listed. The names are all English or Irish – this was a community where immigration from other distant lands was as yet unknown. Among the many parish organizations, the names of office-holders are listed formally, as Miss this or Mr that. The altar servers are listed as 'Messrs D. Crotty (MC), W. Crotty, P. Cowie, B. Groom, H. McCrossan, B. McDermott, M. Muldoon, J. Keenan, P. O'Sullivan, J. Coffrey, D. Sheehan, M. Smith, P. Brittain, R. Coffrey, P. Keenan, J. Carty.' The sacristan was a Miss Davis, and the organists Mr Morgan and Mrs Watt. Mr Kearney was in charge of the Association for the Propagation of the Faith (which meant distributing collection boxes for this international Catholic association, and then arranging for the money to be brought together annually and sent off). There was a Football Club with Mr McMullen as Captain and Mr Cernuschi as Secretary. The choir members (mostly female) are listed as are the church collectors (male) and the School Fund collectors (a much larger team, and mixed). There is an article about the importance of daily Mass, and another about the message of the apparitions of Fatima.

The advertisements almost convey the impression of a group of village shops. This was before the days of supermarkets. R. Smith, of 106 Emmanuel Road, Balham, 'fruiterer and greengrocer' boasts 'Orders delivered daily. Salads fresh daily'. For 'China, glass, hardware, heaters, enamelware, aluminium, paraffin etc.' there is the 'Sternhold Domestic Stores' at 23 Sternhold Avenue, Streatham. It is interesting that paraffin, for use in old-fashioned heating stoves, was still a standard household item. Some of the shops offer services which show evidence that this was still very much a time of thrift and make-do-and-mend: a tailor, N. Kay, in New Park Road, offers 'stocking repairs' (this was when 'nylons' were still a novelty, and of course tights had yet to make their appearance), and Henri Mittaux of Park Road is a 'specialist in knitting wools' for a community where many women still evidently knitted their own and their families' socks and jerseys. A bicycle shop, P. A. Fern offers 'repairs a speciality'.

Now that the annual parish garden fete, and the Christmas bazaar, both of which had of course ceased during the war years, had been revived, funds started to come in for the parish school, and the 'outdoor collection' was also re-established. Much of Clapham Park – as much of Britain generally – had a shabby air as wartime austerity and the difficulty of getting building materials made it hard to carry out repairs and renewal of buildings. The presbytery at St Bede's – Hyde House – was in a very poor state and many of the rooms were filled with junk that had accumulated over the years.

In early 1952 Fr Hooley's health began to fail, and in March he died. He had been parish priest at St Bede's for forty-three years and his loss was very keenly felt. An era was ending. The curate, Fr Tim O'Driscoll, had to take charge while arrangements were made for Fr Hooley's successor.

Fr Hooley's time at St Bede's stretched right back to the days of tension with Cardinal Bourne, and the time before the First World War. He had overseen the creation of a parish school and the emergence of a large and thriving Catholic community in a bustling suburb.

In April 1952 Fr Gerald Fothergill was appointed to the parish, and worked as parish priest for eighteen months, assisted by Fr O'Driscoll. Then in 1954 Fr Fothergill was appointed to the bigger and busier parish of Littlehampton on the Sussex coast, and was replaced at St Bede's by Fr John O'Connor.

It was now nearly ten years since the end of World War Two and it was possible to build and see a time of real prosperity ahead. Finally, the enormous efforts for fund-raising and the heroic efforts of the parish to establish its own school were to see results. Much of the money had come from the parishioners' own efforts, and there was also to be money from public funds – but to achieve this had been a long battle. Local Catholics saw this as a matter of fighting for justice – under the law they were entitled to a Catholic school for their children, and in addition to paying a large amount of the money needed for this they were surely entitled, like all other citizens, to the use of facilities provided through taxes and rates. Now a new St Bede's Junior Boys School was opened, with places for 160 boys.

The managers first met on 19 December 1957 under the chairmanship of Mgr Edward Mahoney (who was to be a dominating figure in Southwark diocesan educational policies for many years). The other members of this first small team of managers were Mrs S. C. McAvoy, Mr W. Keenan, and Mr C. J. A. Joyce. The minutes note:

> The Chairman gave a report on the progress of the building work. On the original estimate this was due to finish in July 1958 in which case the school should open in September 1958. He pointed out, however, that the work was behind schedule due to unavoidable delays and that consequently these dates might be changed.

In May 1958 Mr J. Brennan was appointed headmaster, and Mrs M. J. Lang and Mr T. Carty as members of staff. By now Fr O'Connor was the chairman of the managers and despite Mgr Mahoney's grim pronouncements about delays, things were going ahead smoothly. A meeting on 9 February 1958 reported:

> Regarding the building there had been no real troubles. The heating was excellent. A number of windows had been broken by hooligans. On the question of equipment it had been decided to install towel masters instead of roller towels and these were now awaiting fixing. Ample library cupboards were available and these would carry a display of gay books to encourage reading ...

This last sentence is an absolutely classic example of how a word has completely changed in meaning over half a century – sadly, the expression 'gay books' no longer means happy and attractive books but ones which promote a homosexual lifestyle – something utterly unimaginable in 1958.

The school duly opened in the Autumn and by May 1959 had 122 pupils. Four years later in November 1963 it had a formal inspection from one of Her Majesty's school inspectorate. The report gives a flavour of life in Clapham Park at the time. Noting that the school is for boys, it comments:

> Junior girls and infants attend its counterpart, St Bernadette, a short distance away. Although the boys come from fairly widely scattered homes, few have to use public transport and most are within fifteen minutes' walking distance. They are well-behaved, polite, and show themselves eager to work.

The St Bernadette's school for junior girls was in fact unique in its position in these post-war years. It evolved from the (fee-paying) preparatory department of La

51

Retraite School and thus initially came under the same headmistress, although under the 1944 Education Act it was to be State-funded. Named in 1958, for the Lourdes centenary, its first headmistress was Mother Mary Teresa (Sister Ruth Ashworth, now Superior of La Retraite Convent, Salisbury). Some years later, as we will see, this whole arrangement of schools was reorganized, St Bede's School becoming mixed.

Family life was the foundation of parish life at St Bede's. A branch of the Union of Catholic Mothers was established in the parish in 1955. The first President was Mrs Baum, with Isabel Keenan as Treasurer and Aileen Cunningham as Secretary. In those days each committee member was asked to 'bring along a few lumps of coal to keep the Club fire burning'. The group thrived. For many years Mrs Kathleen Shaw was secretary – her daughter was also active in the parish and became a La Retraite nun. In 2003 St Bede's UCM is the largest branch in the diocese. Over the years it has been at the heart of parish activities such as the annual bazaar (raising approximately £7,000 per year). It has run regular pilgrimages to the Marian shrines at Aylesford and Walsingham, together with longer trips to Lourdes.

Meanwhile throughout the 1950s and early 60s there were building improvements around St Bede's. A parishioner recalls:

Fortunately he [Fr O'Connor] came from a building family and was able to see the possibility of making the presbytery a great house again, and set about doing quite a lot of things in a quiet methodical way.

The basement of the house had contained the kitchen and dining room, a very dark wide passage and a room which was the housekeeper's sitting room and the boiler house. These were in a pretty run down state. A stone staircase went up to the main part of the house, where the ground floor was used as parish rooms, and various meetings and events were held there.

While major re-ordering was carried out, parish meetings were held in the school or in the sacristy. Eventually the house was arranged in more or less the form in which it is today.

A parish brochure printed a few years later describes other developments:

A new look was given to the front of the Church and house. To perpetuate Fr Hooley's memory a new stone altar replaced the original wooden one with a very fine stained glass window behind it. During this time Fr O'Connor was assisted by Fr O'Driscoll who in turn was replaced by Fr Edward Adlem in 1956. The very rapid development of our diocese at this time meant an acute shortage of priests and Father Adlem had to be taken for Worcester Park in 1959, leaving the Parish Priest on his own for a time. Father Peter Cassidy, a Columban father, came to assist temporarily. Unfortunately during these last few months Fr O'Connor's health had not been too good and he decided to ask the Bishop for a less arduous parish. In October 1959 he went to Send in Surrey.

The new altar, built in Fr Hooley's memory, was specially ordered from Apuania in Italy, made of Sicilian pearl marble, Algerian onyx and with a centre panel in gold mosaic. The firm concerned wrote at the end of August 1956 to Fr O'Connor, saying that it would be packed in two boxes and should arrive towards the end of September, ready for erection in mid-October.

From 1959 the parish priest was Fr Joseph Sullivan, Monsignor Denis Wall from 1966–67 and in 1967 Fr Ronald Salmon was appointed. There were arrivals and departures of curates too: in 1959 Fr Peter Cassidy arrived, and the following year Fr Cornelius Bodewes who served until 1972 and died in 1973. From 1968–72 Fr Francis Pole was curate. He sadly left the priesthood and indeed the Catholic Church and became an Anglican. In 1972 he was replaced by Fr Paul Sanders.

A parish directory published at the beginning of the 1970s states:

The Parish Priest is Fr Ronald Salmon. He previously served at Dover and in Bermondsey before coming to Clapham Park in 1967. He is assisted by Fr Cornelius Bodewes SMA. Fr Bodewes is Dutch by birth and spent forty years working on the missions in Africa before joining the Parish in 1960.

In St Bede's church itself, various items still in regular use have their own history. The six wrought iron candlesticks that now stand at the back of the sanctuary were given to the church in memory of Fr Hooley and were originally donated as catafalque candles for funerals.

For Catholics, the major event of the 1960s and early 1970s was the Second Vatican Council and its aftermath. Initially seen by its participants as a massive gathering of the world's bishops to celebrate a period of undoubted success and growth in the Catholic Church, the Council became something quite different. While the world's bishops gathered in somewhat celebratory mood, great changes were waiting in the wings.

Most older Catholics today still tend to talk about the new liturgical and other arrangements introduced into the Church following the Second Vatican Council as 'the changes'. Many of these changes were not, of course, what the Council actually wanted or mandated, a situation that will clearly right itself in time. For any Catholic under the age of thirty-five, however, the somewhat chaotic liturgical arrangements which have characterized many parishes, and the sense of confusion in the Church about many fundamental teachings, are seen as quite usual, and it is hard for older people to convey the sense of stability that was a part of Catholic parish life before the events of the late 1960s.

In St Bede's, 'the changes' were possibly less dramatic

than elsewhere. The new English translations of the Mass were used, replacing the old rite in Latin. Popular devotions such as Rosary and Benediction declined. A forward-facing altar was created. Experiments were made with various types of music using guitars and other instruments. None of these affected the beliefs at the heart of the Catholic Faith. But there were also profound debates going on throughout the whole Catholic Church about fundamentals: the Divinity of Jesus Christ, the real meaning of the Mass, the teachings of the Church on marriage and divorce and priestly celibacy. These were difficult times.

A note in the minutes of the St Bede's School Managers for November 1971 gives a hint of the debates:

> The Archbishop has ordered all religious teaching to be once again soundly based upon the Catechism. This will resolve many years of doubt and uncertainty among teachers about the authoritative basis for religious teaching in Catholic schools.

Alas, the Archbishop's words were not heeded in many schools and doubt and confusion continued to rage for another three decades.

Some of the refurbishments of St Bede's church in this era were unhappy. The beautiful old baptismal font, with its attractive decorative carving, was taken out and replaced with a small modern concrete one. One of the confessionals was turned into a small, cramped baptistery-chapel in which the new font was installed. This was to prove unsatisfactory for many reasons – few could cram in around the font, and much of the drama and symbolism associated with a baptism was lost. Many years later the old font – which had been discovered in the garden, doing duty as a tub for plants! – was rescued and restored, and it now occupies a place of honour near the sanctuary, where it once again fulfils its role of providing the Water of Life for new Christians. (The confessional has been restored to its proper use, and the 1970s font is in a cupboard.)

In the early 1970s there was a tendency to refer to all changes in Catholic life as being evidence of growth and renewal, even where this was not really the case, and also to suggest that the idea of building up the parish as a community and of caring for the poor and disadvantaged was a new one. There are faint hints of this in some of the parish publications of this era. But at an everyday level, St Bede's in the early 1970s was, in effect, still running very much as it had always done, and most of its established organizations were of a traditional sort. It boasted a thriving Scout Group with Cub Scouts for the younger boys, a Guide Company and associated Brownie Pack, a Youth Centre for teenagers, and a 'Frances Ellis Club' for older parishioners. The Union of Catholic Mothers was going strong – in the 1970s the President was Mrs Francesca Knight of Radbourne Road and the Secretary Mrs Kathleen Edwards of Telford Avenue – and there was a Sanctuary Guild for men and boys who wanted to be altar servers. This was a parish which, in years that were to prove difficult for the whole Catholic Church, most parishioners still quietly knew that being a Catholic meant loyalty to Church teachings.

Meanwhile, all of life in Clapham Park was being affected by dramatic social changes. Massive immigration into Britain from the West Indies and from the Indian subcontinent meant that Clapham Park became, during the course of the 1970s, a place where people of different races and backgrounds now mixed and lived.

Schools were changing: it was decided at a diocesan level that all Catholic secondary schools in Southwark including, of course, La Retraite would become comprehensive and amid much debate and heartache various schools were closed and others re-organized.

There were other changes too. In the 1960s successive governments in Britain changed the laws relating to fundamental issues: abortion was legalized, divorce was made easier, the laws restricting pornography were effectively abolished. Contraceptive pills and devices were

56

made available and their use was taught and encouraged through schools and the Health Service. There was talk of the 'permissive society' and the emergence of movements for homosexual rights and for the acceptance of cohabitation as a normal alternative to marriage.

In all of this, one small Catholic parish could feel buffeted and tossed about. While two World Wars had not fundamentally affected the family lives and values of the ordinary Catholics of Clapham Park, the intrusion of debates on the acceptability of abortion and contraception certainly did. The dominant role in people's decision-making was played by the television and, to a much lesser extent, other media such as the radio and the popular press: the Church seemed marginalized and its image was very much at the mercy of television producers and commentators.

Everyday parish life, with its Sunday Masses and its weekday gatherings of various Catholic organizations, nevertheless flourished at St Bede's throughout all these years. The church notices on the whole reflect everyday domestic concerns – fund-raising for various causes, and the arrivals and departures of parish personalities. In 1976, for example, there is a report on the Archbishop's Visitation in February, a note about a Disco Dance in the school hall for teenagers over fifteen, and a Parents' Cheese and Wine Evening at St Bernadette's. In May of that year – to take a month at random – a total of 1200 attended Mass on Sunday, and the collection was £244 with a further £317 given to a special collection in aid of the Verona Fathers. There were comings and goings of members of the parish team: in July the parish bulletin announced:

Two well known faces will be leaving us this week. Today Father Sanders takes up his new appointment at Coulsdon and Sister Angela her new appointment as headmistress of the school in Salisbury. Both Father and Sister have given great work to our parish community for the past few years. We pray that God will bless them in their new work with all success and happiness.

Fr John Malley replaced Fr Saunders, who went on to work in Latin America. Later Fr Malley was in turn replaced as curate by Fr Michael Smith (later Archbishop's secretary).

In 1976 Archbishop Cowderoy died and his successor was Archbishop Michael Bowen. The diocese had been altered in Archbishop Cowderoy's time, with the removal of Sussex and part of Surrey to form the new Diocese of Arundel and Brighton. Southwark meanwhile became an Archdiocese and hence the new and grander title of Archbishop. The historian can note that this was perhaps the final victory over Cardinal Bourne and his thwarted scheme to merge Southwark Diocese into Westminster!

By the end of the 1970s, with the election of Pope John Paul II, St Bede's as a parish had existed through several papacies. In 1981 Fr Salmon left and was replaced as parish priest by Fr William Dinan. Fr Richard Moth was appointed curate in 1982 and remembers:

It was a happy parish. This was my first appointment after ordination and I remember it as a busy place – lots of parish visiting and door-knocking!

There was a great emphasis on youth activities – Cubs and Scouts were very strong. There was also a very thriving Youth Club. It was very popular and in addition to all the regular things like music and table tennis, there were adventure weeks in Wales and once in the Austrian mountains – we took a group along together with some youngsters from Thornton Heath parish.

A number of young people met their future spouses at that Youth Club and had their weddings at St Bede's, including Natalie, the daughter of one of the youth leaders David Wilkins. The club had a great atmosphere and was very much a Catholic group: every meeting included a time of prayer, and members would come to evening Mass on Sundays.

Fr Dinan had forged a link with the Mexican College in Rome, and each summer would see the arrival of young Mexican priests, who would help out in the parish while studying English. Life at the presbytery was comfortable, with the domestic arrangements run by the housekeeper, Mrs Bessie Churchill. She had served in the Land Army in the Second World War, and later became Fr Dinan's housekeeper at his parish in South Maidstone, Kent. She had accommodation in an almshouse in Aylesford near Maidstone but came to help out at Clapham Park.

A major event each year was the Christmas Fayre, which raised substantial sums. There was a tradition that the parish priest always ran the bottle stall, and raffled a TV set! A major organizer of the event was Michael Atkinson, who also ran a six-course sit-down dinner for 200 people as part of the event – this was always extremely popular.

In 1983 there was a Deanery Youth Mission which was run by some Redemptorist priests at St Bede's: Fr John Brooks, Fr Ian Mackay and Fr Gabriel Maguire. A team of twelve young people made all the arrangements and preparations. Events were well attended, with 300 young people attending the final Mass.

A team of doctors and nurses went from St Bede's to Lourdes to help take care of sick pilgrims. The group included the Atkinson family whose daughter, Anne, was a nurse. The group met at St Bede's for Mass followed by breakfast in the parish club, and would then set off on the long journey in a minibus. Other leading activists in the parish were Tony and Daphne Frost, active with the youth club.

It was in the 1980s that parishioner Mrs Veronica Pierson started her work with what was to become the Billings Family Life Centre, now in Vauxhall. This was a response to the need to emphasize the Christian message

59

on marriage and family in a society where increasingly this was drowned out by other voices. Teaching natural family planning and offering marriage preparation, the work began in St Bede's parish club before moving to premises of its own.

The parish maintained good ecumenical relations with the nearby Anglican church of St Stephens. Fr Dinan was also chaplain to the local branch of the Multiple Sclerosis Society and on one occasion this involved blessing a brand new ambulance they had acquired.

The parish schools were thriving, with good teachers: Mr Hickey as head of St Bede's boys school and Sister Helen Dunn at St Bernadette's.

When not working, Fr Dinan was a great golfing enthusiast, and many parishioners and other clergy friends joined him in this over the years, so that it was generally agreed that there was in effect a St Bede's Golf Club which was an unofficial part of the parish life.

After Fr Richard Moth left in 1985 – to study Canon Law in Canada and later to return to Britain and in due course to become Vicar General of Southwark Diocese – he was replaced as curate by Fr Will Hebborn. Later another curate was Fr Alastair Warwick, who sadly left the priesthood, and then Fr Stephen Langridge, who came to St Bede's immediately after ordination in 1990 and is now parish priest in the neighbouring parish of Holy Ghost, Balham.

In 1994 Fr Dinan moved to become parish priest of Cheam, before returning to his native Cork. His replacement was Fr Christopher Basden who took up his appointment on 1 October, with a special Mass for the Eve of the Feast of the Guardian Angels, celebrated by Bishop Charles Henderson. Born in Cairo, and ordained in 1979, Fr Christopher grew up partly in Persia (Iran), and was ordained in Wimbledon by the Archbishop of Isphahan, whom he had known since childhood.

Others who have served in the parish in recent years have included Fr Hugh Thwaites, SJ (of whom more later) from 1995 to 1997, and Fr Riederer, SJ (RIP) from 1997 to 2001. The current parish team includes Fr Andrew Southwell, OSB and Fr Armand de Malleray, of the Fraternity of St Peter.

Scouts and Cubs have been a most important part of life in Clapham Park for many years, the Scouts meeting on Friday evenings and the Cub Scouts on Thursdays. The Scouts were begun by a dynamic parishioner, Con Joyce, and through his hard work large numbers of boys have learned Scouting skills, been inspired by the concept of service, and enjoyed the adventure of Scouting. In recent years Michael Cronin, who was a Cub Scout under Con's leadership, has himself taken the leadership role. The Scouts have enjoyed summer camps in places as far apart as Ireland, Rome, France, and the pilgrimage road to Compostella in Spain.

Among other groups that have played a part in parish life in recent years are a team from Miles Jesu, a new international lay movement: they have a base in South London and have helped with youth work and at St Bernadette's School.

Clapham Park has continued to change rapidly. It now has a wide racial mix in which the traditional English/ Irish blend of London Catholicism is only a small part. St Bede's church and school reflect this. African, Caribbean, and various Latin American countries form the background of many parishioners. The parish is rather proud of its cosmopolitan flavour, reflected in any group of people coming and going to church, and in the registers listing those baptized, married, and buried. Today's London is in many ways a reflection of the Empire of which it was once the hub. In 1997 through the hard work of Sister Augustine Ezeh of the Nigerian congregation of the Daughters of Divine Love, the Afro-Carribean Association of St Bede's was begun. Thaddeus Emenonyou has been its President, and has had loyal help from Merceline Aderibigbe, Dorcas Cato and Lloyd Booker. Several times a year the parishioners of St Bede's enjoy the special

61

Festive Masses which incorporate many ethnic musical traditions and instruments.

In the 1990s a large number of immigrants from Latin America arrived, mostly from Colombia and Ecuador. At the time of writing it is estimated that there may be 250,000 Latin Americans in London, of whom only about ten per cent attend the official chaplaincy Masses at Stockwell and elsewhere. Because of this, it has been Fr Christopher's policy to try to minister to those who live locally, with Spanish-speaking priests such as Mgr Leo White (resident at St Bede's 1997–2000), Fr Rav Olazabal – an Argentinian from the Institute of Christ the King – (1998) and Fr Carlos Blanco of El Salvador who came to St Bede's for several holidays. Finally it was decided to have a weekly Mass for the community. The Association of Latin Americans at St Bede's has been helped enormously by Javier Baez, Catalina Snowdon, Conception Barretto, and a committee of loyal and enthusiastic members.

An important part of St Bede's life is the old Latin (Tridentine) Rite of Mass. For many years parishioner Jim Hogan, long-time resident of Kings Avenue had hoped and prayed for the return of the Old Latin Rite at St Bede's, and he requested this several times to the priests. In 1995 his dream was realized with the arrival in the parish of Fr Hugh Thwaites, SJ. This extraordinary priest came from a family with both Jewish and Christian Scientist roots and had converted to the Faith as a young British Army officer shortly before the fall of Singapore in World War Two, after which he was incarcerated as a prisoner of war in the notorious Changi Camp. In the post-war years he became a Jesuit. He was to work in Tooting and in Brixton, notably as a chaplain to foreign students – with many converting to the Faith through his influence. Saddened by the erosion of the practice of the Faith in the modern Church, and echoing the beliefs of Cardinal Ratzinger that 'at the heart of the ecclesial crisis is the problem of the liturgy' Fr Hugh obtained an Indult in 1988 to say the 'Tridentine' Rite of Mass. St Bede's received a definitive permission for this to continue after 1997, and since Fr Thwaites' time at St Bede's there has been a daily Latin Traditional Rite Mass in the parish. This makes St Bede's unique in London. The Sunday Traditional Rite Mass is usually a sung one at least once a month. It attracts supporters from across London including a number of young families. Fr Andrew Southwell and Fr Armand de Malleray of the Fraternity of St Peter now serve the needs of this group – this has been a happy resolution to a pastoral problem, as alas many have been alienated from the Church by the widespread abandonment of the old liturgy.

St Bede's plays a major role in a number of activities in the wider church. The parish always provides a group of children who take part in the annual Rosary Rally which walks through central London in October, carrying a statue of Our Lady from Westminster Cathedral to Brompton Oratory where devotions are held. Parishioners from St Bede's are also among those who take part in the annual international walking Pentecost Pilgrimage from Paris to Chartres, centred on the daily celebration of the Traditional Latin Rite of Mass.

At the heart of a parish community is the school: 'You are the Church of today and the hope of tomorrow', Pope John Paul has said to young people. St Bede's and St Bernadette's schools were reorganized in 1989 after a decision to make them both co-educational. St Bede's became an Infants School under the trusteeship of the Diocese, and St Bernadette's a junior school under the trusteeship of the Sisters of La Retraite. In 1997 Archbishop Michael Bowen opened the Nursery department at St Bede's, and at La Retraite Girls High School the head teacher Maureen Howie fought heroically for the re-establishment of the Sixth Form. As the Sisters of La Retraite gradually diminished in numbers, more lay staff took over at all the schools. But the Sisters continued to give invaluable help and support as school governors – notably Sister Eileen Hewlett. At St Bernadette's Sister Helen retired as head

63

teacher in 1986 being replaced by the school's first male head teacher Mr Keith O' Cruz. In 2001 he retired after fifteen very happy years and was replaced in turn by Mr Tony Board of Roehampton.

The sisters no longer maintain a convent at La Retraite, although the big girls school there still flourishes. The old convent was used for a while as a home for elderly sisters, but was later sold to a group of Spanish nursing nuns. Their presence in the parish is valued and they make a unique contribution in our huge city by nursing the sick and dying every night – deeply appreciated at a time when it is unusual to see such numbers of young and busy Sisters in traditional habits, committed to an apostolate of service and care.

There have been refurbishments to St Bede's and to the presbytery over the years. Because of the latter's size, and the convenience of Clapham Park to London, it has always welcomed visitor priests who need a base from which to study English while helping in a parish. A steady flow of visitors from many parts of the world, especially Africa, has brought many clergy into the life of the parish. St Bede's began as a type of junior seminary a century ago. Because of its size, the presbytery at St Bede's continues to be of service to priests, notably missionaries in training. The missionaries come largely from Poland – they are diocesan priests from the Centre of Missionary formation in Warsaw. They spend part of the year at St Bede's study-ing English and being of service in the parish. The people of St Bede's befriend them and help them in many ways: some are now parish priests in Zambia, Jamaica, Tanzania, and Kenya. Other priests and seminarians have come for pastoral experience, from the Fraternity of St Peter and the Institute of Christ the King.

In addition to all this, two support groups for priests meet regularly at St Bede's: the monthly seminar founded by Fr Paul Hayward (of the Kelston Club in Balham) in 1995, and the Priestly Society of St John Fisher founded by Fr Sean Finegan in 1988.

There have been several vocations to the priesthood and the religious life from the parish. Fr Philip de Freitas was ordained at St Bede's in 1998, adding his name to priests ordained in this church over the years including Fr John Henry and Fr Tony Charlton in the 1970s, all now actively serving in the Southwark Diocese. In 1993 parishioner Elizabeth Lee went from Clapham Park to St Cecilia's Abbey on the Isle of Wight where she is now Sister Eustochium.

The parish club rooms see regular social gatherings to mark special events in the life of the parish. They are also used by other groups – recently Family Days organized by the National Association of Catholic Families and also the Traditional Family alliance to which Dom Andrew is the chaplain, with a picnic lunch and a guest speaker, have been a feature.

Ecumenical relations are not forgotten and the present writer has been a speaker at a St Bede's ecumenical service for Christian Unity week on a January evening when people from other local churches were invited.

The church, with Hyde House standing next door, continues to provide an oasis of green in Clapham Park. In the church entrance, the noticeboard is always crammed with posters and lists announcing various parish events and activities. Outside, both church and presbytery are set back from the road and the trees and lawns of the gardens make a natural space for people to chat after Sunday Mass and for groups to gather for photographs after weddings and christenings.

If someone from 100 years ago were to visit Clapham Park today, he would most certainly be baffled and confused – the place bears no relation at all to the Clapham Park of the early 1900s. Noisy traffic, an enormous racial and cultural mix of people, every sort of lifestyle and attire, many languages being spoken, and home life centred on the supermarket, the television, the car and the mobile phone – all would be confusing to someone peeping in from the early 20th century. Even if he came to

St Bede's on a busy Sunday, when people are pouring in for Mass, he would see much to puzzle him. The clothing would seem bizarre: a typical congregation is mostly dressed – men and women alike – in close-fitting trousers, many in identical blue denim, with a simple open-necked shirt or casual jacket. Formal suits for men are extremely rare and hats for ladies almost unknown. The cars cruising around to find a parking space, the occasional bleeping of a mobile phone, and the almost universal footwear of large sneakers would all seem strange to one who had known travel by tram or on foot, formal manners, elaborate 'Sunday Best' outfits, and shiny boots as the norm among London Catholics.

But if he was there, on Sunday or weekday, to see the Host and Chalice elevated at Mass, or people quietly slipping into a confessional one by one to confess sins and receive absolution, or a couple standing in front of the altar with friends and family gathered around as they exchange their marriage vows, or a baby carried to the font for a baptism, he would not feel at all unfamiliar. Now, as for the past hundred years, parish life revolves around the Mass and the Sacraments at St Bede's. God is worshipped. The Catholic Faith is taught, and children are brought for baptism and later to make their First Confession and First Communion. The Bishop comes to give the Sacrament of Confirmation. The dead are brought for their funeral Mass and the penitent come for confession. People slip in to pray. The priests say the Office. All of this is what Frances Ellis knew was necessary when she first donated money for a church to be built in this small corner of London.

Here, the Faith given to the Apostles is quietly passed on, and souls are fed. Here, as the years unfold, a parish history is written – the ordinary achievements and adventures of the Catholics who happen to live in a particular place at a particular time. St Bede, in his vanished Saxon world, and Frances Ellis, in her vanished late-Victorian one, are in a mysterious sense not far from us when we gather at St Bede's and a priest raises his hand to make the Sign of the Cross as Mass begins. In a Catholic Church, as nowhere else on earth, all history becomes one: here the author of time Himself comes down to be among us.